Needlework Classics

"Perhaps you have one yourself—I have, a little brass bird that perches on the edge of my sewing table and opens an obliging bill to hold my fancy work when I am embroidering." Helen Berkeley-Loyd, Butterick Designs, *1911.*

Needlework Classics

NOSTALGIC DESIGNS FROM THE
BUTTERICK ARCHIVES FOR DECORATING CLOTHING AND ACCESSORIES

Edited by Becky Stevens Cordello

Butterick Publishing

Editor-in-Chief
Becky Stevens Cordello

Associate Editor
Barbara Weiland

Art Editor
Janet Lombardo

Copyright © 1976 by
BUTTERICK PUBLISHING
161 Sixth Avenue
New York, New York 10013

A Division of American Can

Library of Congress Catalog Card Number 75–35417
International Standard Book Number 0–88421–023–5

Butterick Publishing wishes to thank the following individuals who generously donated their time to adapt, interpret, and execute the design samples which appear in color throughout *Needlework Classics*.

Cover: Barbara Weiland, embroidery; Janet Lombardo, filet crochet.
Page 18: Janet Lombardo, embroidery.
Page 20: Elaine Schmidt, punch-work embroidery.
Page 25: Barbara Weiland, braiding.
Page 28: Evelyn Brannon, patchwork.
Page 32: Evelyn Brannon, needlepoint luggage tag, checkbook cover, billfold cover, embroidered buttons; Becky Cordello, needlepoint and beaded evening bag; Carol Gull, needlepoint belt; Marsha McCormick, needlepoint tennis racquet cover; Harriet Sottile, embroidered tie; Barbara Weiland, appliqué tote, braided belt, trapunto evening bag.

In addition we wish to thank Joan Short Originals, Inc. for the ready-made accessories for needlepoint shown on page 32. These items are available at most needlework shops.

Fashion Illustrations by Susan Blackman
Fashion Photography by Bob Jaffe
Still Photography by Laurence Cox
Book Design by Bob Antler

Preface

"Taste and ingenuity, with a very small amount of cash, will enable a lady to appear always fashionably attired . . . no excellence of mind or soul can be hoped for from an idle woman."

Godey's Lady's Book, *1845*.

Distinction in dress has long been of interest as a means of identification and status, and as a statement of individuality. For this reason and for economics as well, a resurgence in home sewing and a revival of the decorative needle-arts have complemented each other in recent times. Needlework on clothing, whether handmade or purchased, is a current, growing trend but not a new one to be sure.

"Embroidery is the mother of all needlecraft, and is truly as great an art as painting or sculpturing. Much of early history is handed down to us by different pieces of embroidery depicting events or persons of ancient times. In olden days the embroiderer was the designer as well and many men devoted their lives and time to this work."

Butterick Designs, *1911*.

In this country, needlework has long been revered as a practical art and an indispensable accomplishment for young ladies of refinement. In the late 1800's a young schoolgirl copied into her sewing notebook these reasons for learning to sew and do needlework:

"1. To train the hand and eye.
2. To quicken observation.
3. To develop independence.
4. To cultivate habits of industry.
5. To inspire respect for intelligently executed work.
6. To study form and color in dress and decoration.
7. To teach a knowledge of the different textile fabrics.
8. The instruction in sewing should correlate with other subjects and form an educational medium. It should fit girls for practical life."

Obviously, needlework was looked upon not only as an art but also as a discipline meant to teach perseverance, independence, industry, and respect for one's own work and that of others.

Today, men and women alike are engaged in the happy pastime of decorating clothing and accessories with imaginative combinations of needlework forms. In our busy lives, needlework is an important creative activity for filling idle moments, for relieving tension, and for stamping individuality on the mass-produced items of our industrial society.

Designing for needlework is a natural extension of one's artistic aptitudes but for those who lack the skills necessary to translate an idea to paper and then to cloth, inspiration and assistance are required. And so, *Needlework Classics* has evolved to inspire and encourage you to creative expression through needlework on clothing. The major portion of *Needlework Classics* is devoted to a collection of over 140 designs carefully chosen from old publications which extolled the virtues of needlework to their readers on a monthly basis. Each of these designs appears in a clear line drawing easily traced directly from the page. The designs were selected for their artistic and historic merit and their suitability for application to clothing. A brief history of each design and suggestions for interpretation are keyed by number to each design. The designs can be used exactly as they appear on the design plates or they may be enlarged or reduced, curved or straightened, segmented or combined in an arrangement perfect for your purposes.

Careful planning is crucial for a successful project. Therefore, complete instructions for this process appear in Part I, "Plan the Perfect Project." You will find additional assistance in project planning in Part II which contains beautiful examples of needlework in color photography and artwork. Complete illustrated instructions for executing your planned projects appear in Part IV, "Needlework Materials and Techniques." The techniques discussed include embroidery, beading, braiding, punch-work, appliqué, patchwork, quilting, trapunto, needlepoint, and filet crochet.

Although the designs which appear in this volume were chosen for use on clothing, many of them originated as patterns for household linens and pillows and are still suitable for these purposes. Remember, too, that many designs planned for one needlework technique can be easily adapted to another. Braiding patterns can be quilted or beaded, patchwork designs can be worked in needlepoint, and needlepoint can be worked from cross-stitch and filet crochet patterns. With a little ingenuity you can adapt a design to any purpose you like. This idea of adaptability and interchangeability was aptly expressed in the early 1900's by a Butterick needlework editor who took her training in the needle-arts in a French Convent School.

"A Frenchwoman would not hesitate to take a pattern meant for half a dozen doilies and use it to trim a new coat suit. . . . She has a mind open to conviction in regard to the good points of anything that is shown her, and she allows herself to be hampered by no conventions. If she prefers to use a towel-end pattern to trim a tunic she will do so quite as unhesitatingly as she would use a tunic pattern for a towel-end if the whim seized her. . . . She shows an endless amount of inventiveness in combining designs, colors, and stitches so that the result is peculiarly distinctive—a thing

that belongs to her alone, and is the work of her head as well as her hands. Generations of convent-school training have made her well-versed in the use of the simplest stitches. The sweetbriar stitches that suggest nothing but flannel petticoats to an unimaginative woman mean to her the sweetest sort of trimming for baby dresses, blouses, and lingerie collar and cuff sets. A chain stitch worked in a heavy-fiber silk saves the expense of the braid that always figures so prominently among a dressmaker's findings."

Helen Berkely-Loyd
Butterick Designs, *1911.*

In selecting this special group of designs we have relied on the rich source of needlework history contained in the Butterick Archives. The majority of the oldest designs were found between the covers of two fascinating Victorian publications, *Peterson's Magazine* and *Godey's Lady's Book* referred to as *Peterson's* and *Godey's* in this text for the sake of brevity. These two publications brought Paris fashion to American women every month in beautiful engravings and hand-colored fashion plates. In addition, each magazine carried serial romances, helpful household hints, music, poems, recipes, and patterns for every imaginable form of needlework. *The Delineator,* a similar publication was first available in 1875. Its primary purpose was to promote Butterick patterns, but it, too, promoted fancy-work patterns to the delight of every avid needlewoman. *The Delineator* was published by Butterick into the 1930's and as the years passed it took on the characteristics of current ladies magazines. Three additional old Butterick publications, *Needle-Arts, Butterick Designs,* and *Butterick Transfers,* promoted Butterick's hot iron transfer patterns for needlework and included instructions for a variety of needlework projects including knitted and crocheted sweaters, sewing basket accessories, filet crochet lingerie, beaded handbags, and embroidered household linens. Several other old Butterick publications provided additional designs.

Needlework Classics is, itself, an heirloom and a rich source of inspiration sure to help you fill free moments with the pleasurable pursuit of creativity in needlework on clothing—or whatever else suits your fancy.

Barbara Weiland

Contents

PART ONE

Plan the Perfect Project 9

The Urge to Embellish 9
Preliminary Planning 10
Design Placement and Adaptation 10
Selection of Materials and Techniques 11
Project Sequence 11
Enlarging and Reducing Designs 12
Transferring Designs to Fabric 12
Blocking 14

PART TWO

Needlework Treasures:

A Peek Into Grandma's Sewing Basket 15

Color Plates 17

PART THREE

The Classic Designs and Their Origins 33

Embroidery 33
Punch-work 54
Beading 58
Braiding 63
Quilting 68
Appliqué 72
Patchwork 81
Needlepoint 86
Filet Crochet 96
Alphabets 100

7

PART FOUR Needlework Materials and Techniques 106

Embroidery   106
Punch-work   110
Braiding   111
Beading   112
Quilting   113
Trapunto   115
Appliqué   116
Patchwork   119
Needlepoint   120
Filet Crochet   124

Index 128

1
Plan the Perfect Project

The Urge to Embellish

Mankind has a long history of decorating the things that are important to him: his home, his body, and his clothing. In our modern times, the urge to embellish clothing reflects both the ancient impulse to decorate and the contemporary need to feel unique in a world full of mass-produced uniformity. It is no surprise that the current symbols of mass-production, the T-shirt and blue jeans, are favorite objects for needlework of every description.

Fashion has seen many changes over the years and materials and tools have developed as well. Needlework techniques and the reasons for undertaking a needlework project have, however, remained essentially unchanged. An 1831 article in *Godey's* dealt with embroidery, and began with these words:

> *"To this art (embroidery) our readers are indebted for some of the most elegant articles of dress. It may, also, afford them opportunities of displaying their taste and ingenuity; and offers a graceful occupation and an inexhaustible source of laudable and innocent amusement."*

Those gracefully expressed ideas are as relevant today as they were 140 years ago.

If the technological advances of the machine age are to be blamed for the decline of style in the 19th century, then the technology of the 20th century can be credited with producing increased leisure time and providing improved needlework materials and as a result, contributing to a revival of popular interest in needlework. In addition, many specialized needlework tools have been developed and are widely and inexpensively available, making satisfactory results easier to attain than ever before. A glance at the nostalgic needlework tools in this book will show you how many changes have been made in this area.

Needlework for clothing can be used in several ways. It may, like embroidery, simply embellish clothing. It may also enhance the function of clothing, like quilting which provides warmth. Or, like patchwork or needlepoint, it may actually form fabric. Whatever its form or function, the methods and skills required will be essentially the same as for working a pillow or a picture, but needlework on clothing will require additional thought and planning.

The following sections cover everything you need to know to get on with the happy experience of embellishing your clothing and accessories with needlework. A discussion of how to choose, adapt, and interpret needlework designs on clothing is followed by procedures basic to all needlework: enlarging, reducing, and transferring designs, and blocking. Following the color and design plates and historical notes, there is a step-by-step guide to the basic techniques for embroidery, beading, braiding, punch-work, needlepoint, patchwork, appliqué, quilting, trapunto, and filet crochet. Also included is information on adapting these needlework forms to the clothing you make or buy.

Preliminary Planning

Many factors influence the ultimate combination of design, needlework technique, and materials which will prove right for a given project. These three areas should be considered simultaneously and must be compatible with the purpose of the garment.

A factor that will greatly influence the choice of technique and materials is *care compatibility.* Since clothing usually requires cleaning more frequently than other needleworked items, every component part of the project must be chosen with the thought "How will I clean it?" and compatible cleaning needs should influence project styling decisions. If the garment is washable but the yarn chosen is not, then the entire project is not washable. You must decide which is more important: washability or the nonwashable element. Preshrink garments, fabrics, and backings for projects in which washability is an important feature and use only colorfast and shrinkproof yarns and threads.

The garment itself will frequently dictate which materials or techniques are desirable. A lightweight chiffon cannot support a heavily beaded design motif; delicate eyelet embroidery would be difficult to stitch on a woolen jacket. Suitability of techniques and materials to the purpose of the garment must be considered. A silver-beaded butterfly would not be practical on an everyday shirt, whereas that same butterfly, appliquéd or embroidered, would be perfect.

Design Placement and Adaptation

The seams and sections of clothing provide many natural and obvious spots for a touch of needlework but the

needlework should appear to be a part of the overall fashion. It must look as if it belongs and not like an afterthought. Since the eye will be drawn to needleworked areas, placement should be done thoughtfully to avoid emphasizing less attractive areas of the body.

The size, shape, and placement of the design must be compatible with the lines and texture of the garment. Since designs on clothing are seen in the round, it is sometimes a good idea to trace the entire design on paper and pin it in place on the garment (or a similar one) for help in visualizing just how the garment will look when completed.

Isolate a single motif in a complex design if the entire design is too large for the chosen garment area. Use it once or repeat it scattered, clustered, or in rows. Use multiple rows of linear designs.

Enlarge or reduce a design or design element. Use various sizes on the same garment. Position larger sizes toward the lower edges of the garment and smaller sizes toward the top. Sometimes a single element can be greatly enlarged to use alone, but too great a degree of enlargement may result in a loss of form and detail. Too much reduction may make the design too small to work. Quilting design enlargements must not leave more than three inches of unquilted area because the filler will slip.

Rearrange the elements of a design. For example, if you want a band to compliment a design you have chosen for a pocket, rearrange the elements of the pocket design.

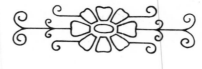

Rearranging must be done with care in order to preserve harmony within the design. Work out the new design on tracing paper.

A straight design can be gently curved. Transfer the design onto tracing paper. Slash, then spread or lap the tracing paper until the desired curve is attained. Trace the new design to another sheet of tracing paper and examine it critically. Fill in broken lines, eliminating any conflicting secondary design elements (often leaves and tendrils) from the lapped section. Add similar elements to balance the spread areas if necessary.

To create a corner, isolate the main element of the design and place it in the corner. Keeping the other elements as unchanged as possible, arrange them on either side of the main motif in the desired angle.

Selection of Materials and Techniques

Each needlework technique has its own personality and the techniques vary in suitability and ease of application to articles of clothing. The needlework technique should be compatible with the design and the end use of the garment.

Since the designs in this book were selected for their versatility, each design can be interpreted effectively in several different needlework techniques. For instance, all of the graph designs are suitable for needlepoint or cross-stitch embroidery. Most of the graphs can also be worked in filet crochet. Many of the motifs in the book can be outlined or filled in with embroidery stitches, beads, or braid. Linear designs can be braided, beaded, or quilted. They can be embroidered in chain or stem stitch. Most patchwork designs can be interpreted in needlepoint or in appliqué. Appliqué designs can be embroidered. The possibilities are endless.

Needlework techniques can be combined for dramatic and unusual effects. Combine beads with needlepoint, embroidery, or quilting for glamour. Embellish appliqués with embroidery stitches or beads.

If you plan to combine needlework techniques, work the one which covers the largest area first. Machine stitching should always be done first. Beading and embroidered details are always done last.

The needlework materials and stitches are the final considerations in planning. Yarn and fabrics provide the color and texture that make a design come alive.

Choosing colors and color combinations is a highly personal matter. The color suggestions given for some of the designs and projects in this book are precisely that, suggestions. The key for the color symbols used on graphed designs in this book appear on page 122. Choose your color schemes based on what the colors say to you. Remember that strongly contrasting colors will have greater impact on clothing than close tones. To plan color combinations for the designs in this book, place a sheet of tracing paper over the selected design plate and clip in place. Trace design lines, then experiment with colors using colored pencils, crayons, or felt tip markers.

Texture is more complex. The yarns and fabrics themselves are textured. Yarns are formed into stitches which create additional textures. The play of the smooth or rough yarn against the fabric is an important consideration; fine, gauzy fabrics are best worked in a fine yarn or floss; bulkier yarns can be used on sturdier, heavier fabrics. A filled-in design will have more color and texture than one which is only outlined in stitches.

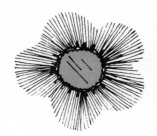

Consider the ultimate use of the garment and select stitches that will wear well. A stitch which is any longer than ⅜″ is not advisable on a garment which will receive hard wear because the stitches might snag or pull. Care must be taken in stitching. Threads should be started and ended securely. Appliqué and embroidery stitches must not be too long or droopy and a hoop should be used whenever possible to help keep the work smooth and the tension even.

It is a good idea to work a small sample using the materials, design, yarns, and stitches chosen if you are at all unsure of their suitability to each other. This sample can also be used to test for washability.

Project Sequence

Whenever possible, needlework designs should be transferred to and worked on flat fabric pieces before the garment is constructed. In the case of a design which goes around a neckline or around a hem edge, seams which the design will cross may be stitched first, then the design worked. This will result in an uninterrupted, finished design. Allowance must also be made for darts and similar construction features. Needlework should be carefully planned to avoid working within these construction areas.

With appropriate care and planning, designs can also be transferred and worked successfully on purchased and other already constructed clothing. Consider the following guidelines for transferring and working needlework on homesewn and ready-made items.

Before Garment Construction

1. Position pattern pieces on fabric; observe grainline. For those pieces which will receive needlework, allow two to three extra inches all around. Pin in place.
2. On pieces to be worked, thread trace seamlines and cutting lines on fabric. See page 13.
3. Cut out, allowing two extra inches all around for most types of needlework. Allow three inches if piece is to be quilted.
4. Work design; clean and block if necessary.
5. Pin appropriate pattern tissue to worked pieces us-

ing thread tracing as a guide for positioning. Cut
away excess fabric following pattern cutting lines.
6. Complete garment construction.

The sections of the garment which will be worked must
be generously cut, as noted in step 3, above, since most
forms of needlework will draw up the fabric affecting its size
and shape. Generous cutting allows for this shrinkage and
makes the pieces large enough to fit into a hoop. It also
facilitates blocking. It is a good idea to buy extra fabric in
anticipation of this need. For most projects, an extra ¼ to
½ yard is ample, but if you are planning all over or extensive quilting or trapunto, buy an extra ¼ yard for each
major pattern piece.

After Garment Construction—Including Ready-made Clothing
1. Open out facings and hems in design areas. Unless
   additional support is desired for the needlework, do
   not work through double layers of fabric.
2. If a design is planned for a pocket, remove pocket,
   work design, then replace pocket.
3. If necessary, open leg and sleeve seams to facilitate
   the use of a hoop. Resew when work is completed.
4. Position needlework alongside, not over thick seam
   allowances.
5. Avoid excess quilting or trapunto on completed garments as the stitching and padding necessary might
   affect the fit of the garment. Select simple designs
   instead.
6. To use a hoop on a small piece such as a pocket,
   securely baste the piece to a larger piece of lightweight fabric. Then stretch in hoop and cut away the
   extra fabric behind the area to be worked. If extra
   support is desired for the needlework, work through
   both layers. After the needlework is completed, trim
   excess backing around the design area.

Enlarging and Reducing Designs

The grid system of enlarging or reducing designs has
stood the test of time for ease and accuracy. It was the
method *Godey's* suggested in 1858 for adapting their designs. With a grid, a design can be translated to any size,
larger or smaller.

Decide how much to enlarge or reduce the design.
Consider the space the design will occupy on the garment.

1. Place a grid of exact squares over the design. This
   grid may be drawn on tracing paper. A shortcut is
   to overlay the original design with transparent
   graph paper or fine wire screen. The design may
   also be traced onto graph paper eliminating the
   need to construct grids.

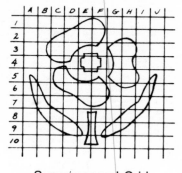

Superimposed Grid

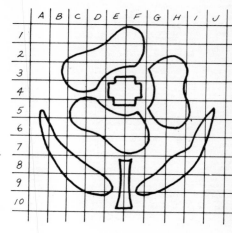

Translating Design
To New Grid

2. Prepare another grid with the same number of
   squares as the first grid. Number the squares along
   the side and letter the squares along the top of both
   grids for easy reference while drawing. Construct
   grids carefully since precision is important to an
   accurate size adjustment.
To enlarge design: The prepared grid should have larger
   squares than the original design. For example, if the
   design to be enlarged is superimposed with a grid
   of ⅛" squares, translate it onto a grid of ¼", ½" or
   1" squares.
To reduce design: The prepared grid should have smaller
   squares than the original design.
3. Translate outline to grid one square at a time. Follow design carefully, checking square by square as
   you go.

Designs may also be enlarged or reduced directly from
the book by "photostating", a photographic process that
produces a negative image or a positive image in matte or
glossy finish. Ask for a positive image because it is easier
to use and a matte finish because it is usually less expensive.
If you would like to reverse the direction of the design, ask
for a "reverse image". You will receive both your original
design and the finished "stat". Find a source for photostating by checking the yellow pages of your phone directory
under "photocopying".

Transferring Designs to Fabric

Methods for transferring designs to fabric have
changed little since *Peterson's Magazine* offered carbon paper
to its readers in 1889, at 15¢ a sheet. Early needleworkers
also used thread tracing and direct tracing when appropriate.

There are a few things about positioning and transferring designs which are unique to clothing and should be
considered before you begin.

☆ When a motif is used on both halves of a garment, one side must be transferred with the design reversed or "flopped" so that the design will be positioned symmetrically on both sides of the garment.

☆ Motifs must be positioned so that they do not extend into the seam allowances; braided designs may extend into the seam allowances but the design should continue uninterrupted when the seams are sewn. On fabric which is entirely quilted the design will also extend into the seam allowance.

Transfer Methods

Supplies
Dressmaker's carbon, dressmaker's chalk pencil.
Do not use ordinary carbon paper. Dressmaker's carbon paper is designed for use on fabric and is available in a range of colors. Choose a color close to your fabric color.
Pencil, stylus, or tracing wheel.
Tissue paper.
Tracing paper.

Dressmaker's Carbon Tracing
1. Trace design onto tracing paper.
2. Tape fabric to hard, flat surface or pin to cutting board with right side up. For ready-made garments place a hard-surfaced item (book or magazine) directly under the area to be marked and pull fabric taut around it. Use a piece of cardboard in pants legs and sleeves. Firmly stuff three-dimensional items like shoes, bags, or hats, with towels or tissue paper.
3. Position design on fabric and secure with pins on two adjacent sides.
4. Slip dressmaker's carbon between fabric and design. Be sure to place waxed side on carbon paper next to fabric. On some fabrics like satins and suedes, the pressure of the tracing wheel will leave a mark without the use of carbon.
5. Go over all design lines with pencil, stylus, or tracing wheel. Check to see if enough pressure is being applied to transfer the design to the fabric. Start at the top and work down to prevent smudging the

lines with the pressure and movement of your hands. Use the pencil or stylus for complex designs and the tracing wheel for simple designs.
6. Remove carbon, pins, and tape. On dark or lightly napped fabrics go over the carbon marks with a dressmaker's chalk pencil or thread trace all lines to insure permanency of marking (see thread tracing below).

Direct Tracing On Tissue Paper Or Sheer Fabric
This is an excellent method to use on clothing and is particularly suited to linear designs worked in beading, braiding, quilting, and embroidery. Use this method on ready-made garments which cannot be carbon traced. If permanent, additional support is needed in a design area, use a sheer fabric like voile or organdy for tracing in place of tissue paper.

1. Trace design directly onto tissue paper or fabric.
2. Baste tissue to fabric with design properly positioned. Baste tracing on sheer fabric to underside of design position.
3. Work design through fabric *and* tracing which serves as a guide and prevents puckering.
4. To remove paper when work is completed, gently pull both sides of paper at same time for a clean tear. If sheer fabric tracing was used, trim away excess fabric around worked design and pink or overcast edges.

Hot Iron Transfer Pencil
These pencils make the ease of hot iron transfer available to the needleworker who wants to use designs other than those available for hot iron stamping. The pencils are available in needlework and craft shops.

1. Trace design onto tracing paper.
2. Draw over back of design with hot iron transfer pencil. Use a fine point.
3. Transfer design to fabric following instructions with pencil. Press slowly with heat suitable for garment fabric. Lift a corner of the design to check for adequate transfer.

Thread Tracing
Use thread tracing where other marking methods would permanently mar the fabric.

1. Trace design onto tissue paper.
2. Position design on right side of fabric and pin or baste in place (for napped fabrics, work from the wrong side of the fabric).
3. Outline the design with running stitches made through tissue paper and fabric.
4. When marking is completed, gently tear the tissue away.

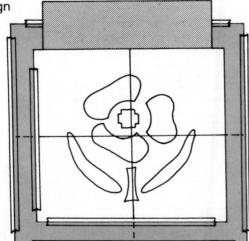

Positioning Design
And Carbon
For Tracing

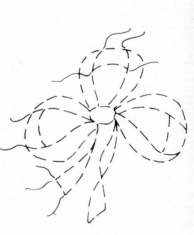

Thread Tracing

Templates

Transferring with templates has remained virtually unchanged since the early days of patchwork. Use templates in needlework such as appliqué, quilting, and patchwork where motifs are repeated.

Templates can be made of brown paper, oak tag, or sandpaper. The design template should be durable enough to use several times. When the edges become frayed, bent, or crumpled, discard the templates because accurate marking will be impossible.

To make a template, draw or trace each design shape on graph paper. Use a ruler to ensure accuracy. Cut out graph paper shapes and glue them onto template material. Cut out template. Accuracy in measuring, transferring, and marking are essential. For most hand appliqué, machine appliqué, and patchwork, use templates in the following manner.

1. Make two templates. One template should be a duplicate of the design and the other template the design plus seam allowances. (Seam allowances for patchwork and appliqué are usually ¼″ or ⅜″ wide).
2. On fabric, trace around largest template first.
3. To mark seam allowances, center the other template within the marked area and trace around it. For some machine appliqué, appliqué with fusibles, and quilting, no seam allowance or turn-under allowance is required.

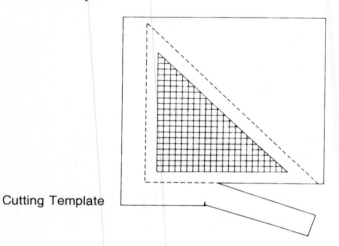

Cutting Template

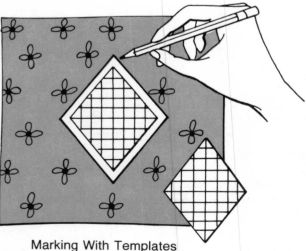

Marking With Templates

Blocking

Blocking is an important finishing step for most needlework projects. It serves to restore the background fabric to its original or desired shape. It helps to even out the stitches and in the case of needlepoint, adds an element of smoothness to the finished piece.

In many cases, especially on small pieces and lightly worked pieces, pressing with steam is sufficient for blocking. On ready-made clothing, this may be the only practical method. A steam iron or damp pressing cloth may be used.

Blocking With Steam—Recommended for embroidery, beading, braiding, punch-work, appliqué, trapunto, filet crochet.
1. Place work face down on thickly padded surface (several layers of terry toweling).
2. Steam press using light pressure.
3. For patchwork, press lightly from wrong side stretching seams slightly to reduce puckers and even out tension.
4. For quilting, hold steaming iron over quilted areas. Do not touch iron to fabric. Smooth fabric with fingers.

When background has been heavily worked or is badly stretched out of shape, blocking on a board will be necessary.

Blocking On A Board—Recommended for heavily beaded or embroidered pieces, needlepoint.
1. Cover a soft wooden board with brown paper or blocking cloth to protect the needlework from stains in the wood.
2. Mark the exact dimensions of the needlework on the blocking surface with a pencil. Check with a T-square to square corners.
3. Stretch piece to match the markings, and tack it to the board. Always use rustproof thumbtacks or push pins. Tack one edge at a time working from the center to each corner. Stretch needlepoint, filet crochet, and flat embroidery right side down. Stretch beading and heavily textured embroidery right side up.
4. Sponge the work with warm water and allow to dry at least 24 hours (up to two days for needlepoint).

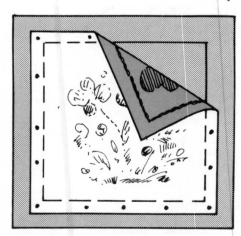

Blocking Needlework

2
Needlework Treasures:

A Peek Into Grandma's Sewing Basket

In "Grandmother's" attic you may find a treasure or two and if sewing and needlework are a primary interest, your gleanings from the attic could include the special tools and implements which gentlewomen once kept in their work boxes or sewing baskets. They are truly beautiful and worthy of collecting as evidenced on the accompanying color plate, page 17. The attic is the first place to search, then antique stores and junk shops if you really wish to pursue a collection. The tools shown here are but a small sampling of the delights of the sewing basket and certainly should develop a reverence for beautiful workmanship which is not always characteristic of today's needlework implements.

1. Black Lacquer Chest for Sewing and Netting Implements, ca. 1790, from the Butterick Archives. This beautiful hand decorated chest was probably brought to the port of New Bedford, Massachusetts during whaling ship days from the China Coast. The box is fitted with carved ivory implements including thimbles, threadwinders, bobbins, needles, thread barrels, gauges and a bodkin.

2. Tape Measure and Emery Cushion in Carved Vegetable Ivory Holder, ca. 1850, from the collection of Ms. Barbara Weiland. Emery cushions are often mistaken for pincushions. Rather, they are small cushions filled with fine emery powder. Needles were thrust into the cushion before use to remove rust and stains and to sharpen the point.

3. *The Dressmaker and Milliner,* 1895. A Butterick publication, this magazine was published quarterly in three languages and illustrated for the dressmaker the latest mode in costuming and millinery in colors and tints.

4. Iron Sewing Bird with Heart-Shaped Clamp, ca. 1740, from the collection of Ms. Elaine Schmidt.

7. Brass Sewing Bird with Clamp and Two Pincushions, ca. 1853, from the Butterick Archives.
The sewing bird evolved from a clamp and was devised to hold material to a table to keep the work firm for sewing. In each of these examples, a clamp is surmounted by a small bird whose beak opens to receive the needlework when the tail is depressed. The first of these was probably made by a local blacksmith and is truly beautiful in its simplicity of line.

5. Beaded Pincushion, ca. 1880, from the collection of Ms. Barbara Weiland. Pincushions of every imaginable size and shape abounded during the Victorian era. This one, handmade of velvet and heavily beaded, is a good example of the late Victorian penchant for making them into free-standing ornaments, often for the dressing table.

6. Wooden Sewing Box, ca. 19th Century, from the Butterick Archives. This velvet-lined, rosewood box, complete with curtained mirror, is fitted with a thimble, and ornate gold scissors, crochet hook, stiletto, and needlecase. The stiletto had a variety of uses including stab-

bing holes for eyelets and unpicking stitches.

8. Hand Embroidered Sample, ca. 1900, from the Butterick Archives. A practice piece for crewel work, this sample is worked in silks.

9. Mother of Pearl Reel Holder, ca. 1830, and M. Heminway Silk Thread, ca. 1876, from the collection of Ms. Barbara Weiland. In the early Victorian days, thread was sold on wooden reels much the same as it is sold on spools today. But the reels were not pretty enough to be seen in a sewing box so holders like this one were developed, the base and top joined by a metal tube which could be pulled apart to accommodate the reel.

10. Sterling Silver Scissors, ca. 1890, from the Butterick Archives. No work box is complete without at least one pair of scissors, but old sewing scissors may be difficult to locate as they are one sewing implement which never went out of use.

11. Sterling Silver Scissors in Sheath, late 19th Century, from the collection of Ms. Elaine Schmidt.

12. Steel Scissors in Stork Design, 20th Century, from the Butterick Archives. Made by Solingen, this pair of sewing scissors is a replica of early Victorian scissors.

13, 14, 16, 17, 18. Handmade Sewing Case and Implements, ca. 1903, from the Butterick Archives. This case (16) was carefully constructed of brown patent leather, then lined in blue silk. It has a small pincushion, needle-book, and thimble holder attached inside. Instructions for a box similar in design appeared in an 1892 issue of Butterick's magazine, *The Delineator.* The existing case is fitted with gold scissors in a sheath, a gold punch or stiletto, and a gold bodkin, thimble, and tape measure (18). An emery cushion (17), and pearl-handled crochet hook (13) and penknife (14) complete the sewing kit.

15. Gold Thimble, ca. 1903, from the Butterick Archives.

19. Heart-Shaped Velvet Pincushion in Sterling Holder, 1891, from the family of Mrs. Laurence Cox. This pincushion was the gift of a sweetheart. It is inscribed "To M. W. W. From A. D. P., March 26, 1891." The recipient was Miss Moriah Watson Williams, a prominent citizen of Utica, New York.

20. Brass Thread Picker, ca. 1890. This "expectant" stork was used as a sewing implement but was probably originally intended for a sugar tongs. A tiny human infant can be found in the stork's stomach when the handles are opened.

21. The Butterick Building at 161 Sixth Avenue, N. Y. C. as it appeared in 1904.

22. Milk Glass Darning Egg, ca. 1830, from the collection of Ms. Barbara Weiland.

23. Wooden Darning Egg, ca. early 20th Century, from the collection of Ms. Elaine Schmidt. This well-worn darning egg unscrews at the middle to reveal a multiple thread reel for storing darning cotton close at hand.

24. Steel Sewing Machine, ca. 1880, from the Butterick Archives. Hand painted gold decoration adorns this little machine, a sewing collector's delight.

25. Brass Pig Tape Measure, ca. 1880, from the Butterick Archives. A tiny delight, the cotton tape winds and unwinds by twisting the little pig's tail.

26, 27. Shuttles for Tatting, ca. 20th century, from the collection of Ms. Elaine Schmidt.

28. Coquilla Nut Wax Box, ca. 1890, from the Butterick Archives. Wax was a necessary material in all sewing boxes until the late 1800's when smooth, machine-made thread became readily available.

29. Thimbles, from the Butterick Archives and the collection of Ms. Barbara Weiland. The gold thimble at the top of the group is from Ms. Weiland's collection. It was a 50th Wedding Anniversary Gift in 1867 and was presented to the owner in a leather-bound case. Silver and brass thimbles in the grouping are from the Butterick Archives and are of late Victorian (1880–1900) design. The carved ivory thimble, ca. 1790, is from the Chinese lacquer sewing chest described above.

30. Ivory Thread Winders, ca. 1790, from the Butterick Archives.

31. Sterling Silver Thread Winder, ca. 1890, from the collection of Ms. Barbara Weiland.
Thread winders have been in use over a long period of time. They are small, flat, many-pointed pieces of ivory, silver, or wood used for winding off lengths of thread for sewing and embroidery, especially silk thread which was most often purchased in skeins.

32. Cranberry Glass Scent Bottle With Gilt Filigree, ca. 1870, from the Butterick Archives. This small item was often found in a sewing box not only for its feminine fragrance, but also to cool the hands with the rapid evaporation of the perfume and to remove grease from the fingers.

33. Wooden Needle-case, ca. 1870, from the collection of Ms. Barbara Weiland. This little barrel is marked, "Accept my best wishes," and is fashioned so that needles of various sizes may be extracted through a hole in the lid when the top of the case is turned.

34. Hand Carved Ivory Needle-case, ca. 1800, from the collection of Ms. Barbara Weiland.

35. Acorn-shaped Needle-case of Vegetable Ivory, ca. 1880, from the Butterick Archives. The loss of a needle was a true catastrophe and since needles were so precious, a variety of beautiful needle-cases appeared. The carved ivory case shown here was designed to be worn from a belt or around the neck on a ribbon or chain.

36. Brass Tape Measure, ca. 1880, from the Butterick Archives. This high-topped shoe is marked, "Three Feet In One."

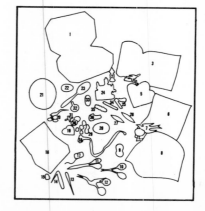

Butterick Quarterly, 1927.

The daisy is a timeless floral design featured here on linen pants in embroidery with various yarns and stitches. This design was adapted from the side pattern for a headdress (cap) featured in *Godey's* in 1831.

The embroidered pocket on the blouse is from *Godey's*, 1863. This exact pocket was given in the magazine in keeping with the "present fashion making the pocket sufficiently ornamental to become a part of the trimming of a dress." Silk embroidery in satin stitch was suggested, with an additional suggestion to place such pockets on the ends of a sash. The pocket featured in the photograph was worked with six-strand cotton embroidery floss.

In 1927, *Butterick Quarterly* showed this organdy fashion described as "the charming mode of the young and slender". That summer, bare arms and low waists were fashionable. The tiny stemless daisy was characteristic of many prints and appeared on even the most formal afternoon or evening dresses.

Design Plate, page 36.

Design Plate, page 69.

Scroll-like shapes have lent themselves to various needle-work interpretations throughout the years, possibly because the non-representational nature of the designs are easy for the less skilled needleworker to execute in a variety of needlework forms ranging from appliqué to outline and braid embroidery.

This 1910 motif from *Butterick Designs* was worked in elegant trapunto on the yoke of a yellow knit dress and is remarkably similar to the embroidered, braided design which accented the "Ulster" coat from 1874. The coat, part of a "modish travelling costume", featured back fullness which smoothly covered a bustle skirt, considered the mode of the day. Of particular interest is the pocket on the coat sleeve, designed with the needs of the traveler in mind.

The Metropolitan, 1874.

Design Plate, page 56.

As noted in the above article from the June, 1859 issue of *Godey's*, the shawl has always been a favorite feminine fashion accessory as it can be worn in a variety of ways to suit the whim of the wearer. It is also a most suitable ground for many lovely forms of needlework as illustrated in the color photo. This heirloom shawl is fashioned of cotton gauze fabric embellished with embroidery and punch-work, an interesting form of pulled-thread embroidery popular from 1910 to 1920. The design chosen first appeared in a 1911 issue of *Butterick Designs* along with the historic figure whose newly fashionable skirt is accented with a blouse featuring a slightly dropped neckline, flowing sleeves, and fullness at the waist held in by a peplum. The punch-work is surrounded by embroidered morning glories.

Butterick Designs, 1911.

For many years braiding prevailed as a very important form of needlework for the decoration of clothing. Essentially, braiding is the couching of cords to fabric in a decorative pattern. On this "walking dress for the sea shore" from an 1845 issue of *The Ladies' National Magazine,* a "beautiful trimming in cord, of a fanciful pattern, reaches up the front of the dress and ornaments the corsage." Milady is the height of fashion in a narrow waist (blouse), ringlets framed by a closefitting bonnet, and her petticoat-stiffened skirt (as many as seven were worn to shape skirts which measured as much as ten yards around).

The shape of the cording design on this dress inspired a contemporary interpretation of a braiding design from a slightly later period, 1859. The original appeared in *Godey's* and was designed for use on a mantle, a fashionable sleeveless cloak. The interpretation here combines couched cording with chainstitch embroidery in bold colors.

The Ladies' National Magazine, 1845.

Design Plate, page 65.

Needle-Art and Transfers, 1927.

The *Needle-Art and Transfer* books of the 1920's were filled with designs which could be purchased for hot iron transfer stamping. In addition, there were knitting and crochet patterns and instructions for crafts such as basketry, silk flowers, and stenciling. Linear designs suitable for interpretation in beading, braiding, or quilting were featured in abundance.

The contemporary figure on this page wears a warm, quilted satin jacket which shows graduated sizes of a 1926 braiding design. This particular design appeared in the book for several years and in 1927 was illustrated on the sleeves of a tubular-shaped clutch-coat in a bold, braided interpretation.

Design Plate, page 70.

Although appliqué as a technique for decorating clothing was not as widely used as braiding and embroidery, this 1899 beauty from *The Delineator* wears an appliquéd trumpet-shaped skirt of "soft cloth". Her highnecked black velvet jacket is adorned with jet beads which delighted Victorian ladies.

The shapes used in the appliqué, so common in clothing decoration, appeared again in a 1919 design for beading from *Butterick Transfers.* The design has been interpreted on a contemporary pants outfit using two different needlework forms: shadow appliqué accents a sheer crepe scarf and braiding sets off an otherwise plain suede pants suit.

The Delineator, 1899.

Design Plate, page 62.

Cross-stitch on gingham is an old favorite widely used on children's clothing and linens. Inspired by a "Ladies Working Toilette" (from an 1891 *Delineator*) with the puffed shoulders and high neck of the era, our contemporary version illustrates that cross-stitch need not be confined to the kitchen. The design on the blouse was one of a series of Butterick *Needle-Art* covers designed for interpretation as cross-stitch samplers. This one is from the Winter 1924–25 issue and showed a couple kissing under the mistletoe. The design has been interpreted here in the original colors cross-stitched on the garment fabric using needlepoint canvas as a guide for stitch uniformity. Complete instructions for this technique appear on pages 109 and 110.

The design is also shown in needlepoint on the canvas flap of a specially designed, ready-made shoulder bag.

Design Plate, page 91.

The Delineator, 1891.

The Delineator, 1885.

Many old braiding designs consisted of simple geometric arrangements done in multiple rows of soutache along the edges of garments. Elaborate variations were also found centered on jacket backs or bodice fronts. The tailored figure from an 1885 *Delineator* illustrates a typical example of this braiding style. The skirts of the era were rather close-fitting and elaborately braided. Bustles were evolving to pulled up puffs in the back and, by the end of the 1880's, had disappeared completely.

Many braiding designs in *Butterick Transfers* were of a geometric nature, too. A braiding design from 1916 which appeared in a section captioned "smart trimmings to make smart dresses smarter" is interpreted here in metallic cording and creates a sophisticated gown for evening in synthetic shantung.

Design Plate, page 65.

Godey's, 1855.

Design Plate, page 42.

For many years, children were dressed like little adults. Basic fashions and needlework designs were scaled down to a more suitable size but there were few needlework designs especially for children's clothing. The lass pictured above from *Godey's*, 1855 wears a typical party dress from this era made of broad bands of English embroidery worked on white cambric. Her pantalets were fashionable for big girls, too.

English embroidery, or "Broderie Anglaise" was an important form of eyelet and satin stitch embroidery which was widely used for petticoat borders, caps, and hankies. It created delicate effects but was time-consuming work and required a certain degree of skill. The designs ranged from simple, graceful ones to those which were elaborate and often overdone (perhaps to show off one's skill).

This petticoat border from *Peterson's* Centennial Volume is a lovely example of the best of the many borders which appeared in the early fashion magazines. Worked on lightweight linen in six-strand cotton embroidery floss, it enhances a beautiful summer jacket.

The stylized plume was a favorite design motif of the Victorian era. The figure below from *Godey's,* 1863, wears an outfit "very suitable for travelling" which featured the plume around hems, cuffs, and pockets, and down the sleeves. This particular design was stamped to look like embroidery, an innovation of the developing American fabric industry. The full-skirted, crinoline-supported silhouette remained popular as well as the full-shouldered, sloping dolman-like sleeves.

Taking its cue from history, a modern interpretation shows a similar plume design gracing the sleeves of an elegant, understated wool crepe dress in satin stitch embroidery. The design first appeared in an 1872 issue of *Peterson's Magazine.*

Godey's, 1863.

Design Plate, page 49.

The strong diamond-shaped border of the 1863 *Peterson's* skirt shown below was the inspiration for a contemporary border interpretation of a patchwork design from an 1859 issue of *Godey's*. The skirt was trimmed with black velvet, either appliquéd or pieced. Worn with a black velvet cloak (the fullness of sleeves during this period made cloaks, shawls, and mantillas necessary) and a plumed bonnet, it was a striking outfit indeed.

More down-to-earth but no less dramatic is the modern jumper with its patchwork band. This fascinating patchwork design was interpreted in chintz and cotton broadcloth and worked in blocks arranged to form a complex, undulating curve.

Peterson's, 1863.

Design Plate, page 85.

Lace has long been a favorite form of needlework for enhancing clothing. In 1859, *Godey's* commented that in no other area "is female extravagance in dress carried to greater length than in the use of elegant and costly laces." Until lace-making machines were invented in the 1850's, lace was handmade abroad and, of course, expensive and difficult to obtain. When American women began to crochet in earnest in the 1860's, they created a lace of sorts which varied in delicacy depending on the yarn used. It was known as filet crochet and was at first used primarily on household articles but during the early part of the twentieth century it was used extensively on clothing, especially lingerie.

Lace insertion like that pictured on the lass from a 1902 *Delineator* is easy to imitate in filet crochet for collars, cuffs, and banding as shown on the contemporary costume. The historic figure appears here in the corseted, sway-backed silhouette of the peroid. The dipped waistline and long puffed sleeves were also typical of the time.

The Delineator, 1902.

Design Plate, page 97.

Household accessories of every imaginable size and shape were the target for Victorian needlework. Patterns for doilies, anti-macassars, cushions, lambrequins, fire screens, and table scarves were the source of many beautiful designs which today may be adapted to clothing or used on household items as originally intended.

An old Butterick publication from 1890 entitled *Needle-Craft* devoted a whole chapter to tables and table scarves and was the source of the design used on the contemporary fashion below. The original velvet table scarf was embroidered in the Kensington stitch (outline or stem stitch), the most popular embroidery of the period. The modern version of the design is gently curved to fit the skirt and blouse yokes and is worked in crewel yarns in outline and satin stitches.

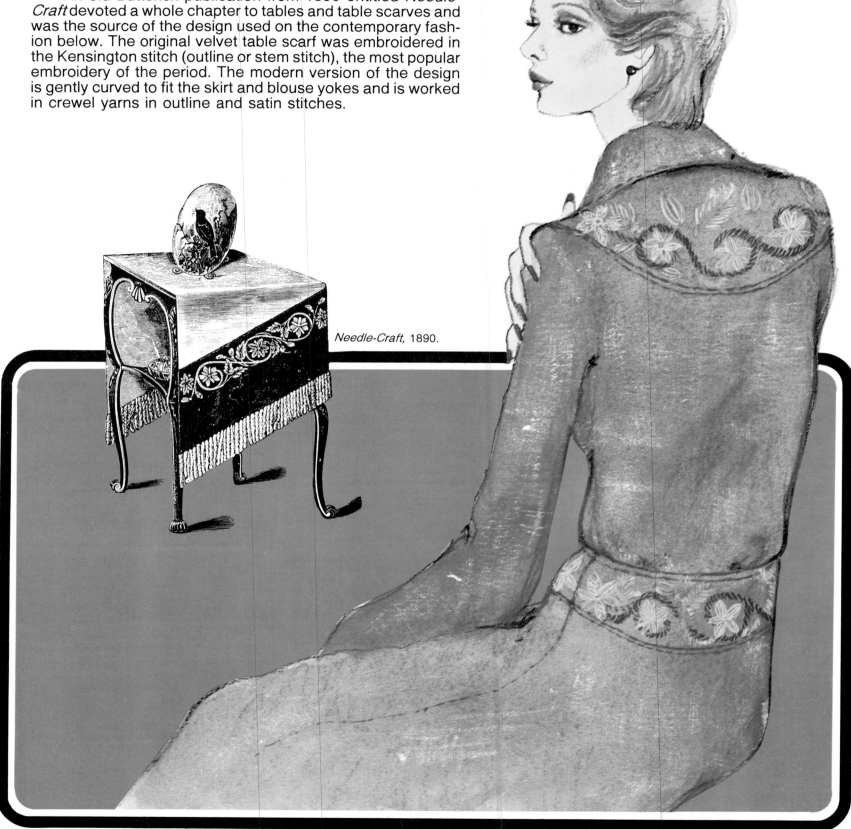

Needle-Craft, 1890.

Design Plate, page 42.

Needle-Art and Transfers, 1926.

In 1926, *Needle-Art and Transfers* showed the gown above with its delicate beaded motifs. Waistlines were still low but the fullness was new and uneven hemlines were extremely fashionable that year. They were considered graceful and easier to wear than an even hemline, combining "the greater elegance of a long skirt with the youthful quality of the short frock." The bolero-effect bodice was another important fashion and it returns in the contemporary fashion illustrated to the left.

The beading design in bugle and seed beads is from *Butterick Transfers,* 1913, and it was originally intended for embroidered banding. It is, however, a beautiful design for beading, as interpreted here on silk crepe reminiscent of the heavily beaded favorites of the flapper period.

Design Plate, page 60.

1. Appliqué Tote Bag, Design 71, page 64. 2. Needlepoint and Beaded Evening Bag, Design 118, page 92. 3. Needlepoint Tennis Racquet Cover, Design 104, page 82 and Design 139, page 102. 4. Needlepoint Billfold, Design 137, page 99. 5. Needlepoint Checkbook Cover, Design 128, page 98. 6. Embroidered Buttons, Design 40, page 51. 7. Needlepoint Luggage Tag, Design 116, page 91. 8. Trapunto Evening Bag, Design 85, page 69. 9. Braided Belt, Design 78, page 66. 10. Needlepoint Belt, Design 115, page 90. 11. Embroidered Tie, Design 138, page 101.

3

The Classic Designs and Their Origins

EMBROIDERY

For many years, embroidery was the primary method for decorating clothing, accessories, and household linens. Embroidered bands for dresses, appliqués for ball gowns, and borders for petticoats were turned out regularly, along with bedspreads, chair seats, and other household items like cross-stitch carpets and bargello upholstery. The eventual easy availability of printed fabrics and machine-made embroidered trims and laces reduced the need and desire to beautify items with hand embroidery.

Embroidery is again popular as a means of adding individuality to mass-produced and hand-made clothing. Almost any item made from or covered with fabric becomes a bit more special with well positioned, well rendered embroidery. The embroidery method chosen will depend on the fabric, the purpose of the garment, and the personal wishes of the needleworker. Many of the embroidery designs which follow are suitable for interpretation in other needlework forms, particularly beading and needlepoint.

Design Plate, page 36.

1. *Godey's,* 1831. This design was the side pattern for

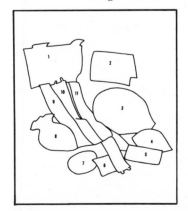

a headdress, a predominant style of the period. It is suitable for embroidery in a variety of stitches including eyelets and lazy daisy in various yarns as worked on the casual, ready-made slacks which appear on page 18.

2. *Godey's,* 1863. For a contemporary look, construct this pocket as one piece and outline the flap in a "fool-the-eye" effect as shown in color on page 18. Embroider in French knots, lazy daisy, outline, and satin stitches.

Design Plate, page 37.

3. *Peterson's,* 1882. This design for the toe of a flannel bath slipper appeared in the December issue of *Peterson's.* The leaves were satin-stitched in two shades of any color, the connecting lines in gold-colored silk. Try it on a handbag or use in a smaller size for a blazer pocket.

4, 5. *Godey's,* 1830. Throughout 1830, *Godey's* presented an installment series on embroidery which was later compiled into one long article. These flowers were illustrations of embroidery on net to imitate lace. The simple shapes invite experimentation with a variety of interesting stitches and yarns.

Design Plate, page 38.

6. *Godey's,* 1831. Embroider this band on seams and edges in French knots, satin, and outline stitches. Enlarge

it for appliqué with brightly colored felt flowers and mirror embroidery centers.

7. *Butterick Designs,* 1910. These stylized chrysanthemums were suggested for satin stitch and seed stitch embroidery on skirts and coats. Color on color would be lovely in this elegant design. Pad leaves for extra richness.

8. *Peterson's,* 1859. This handkerchief border appeared for embroidery on muslin or cambric. It is suitable for outline or satin stitch embroidery and need not be confined to the lightweight fabrics for which it was originally designed.

Design Plate, page 39.

9. *Butterick Designs,* 1911. This delicate design, originally intended for an embroidered pillow top, is especially suited for embroidery on the bodice of a simple blouse or dress. A pillow would be equally lovely worked in this pattern.

Design Plate, page 40.

10. *The Delineator,* 1892. This graceful feather first appeared as feather stitch embroidery for pillows, scarves, and other household items. Bows of baby ribbon were appliquéd after the embroidery was completed. Work in silk or fine gold metallic thread on a chiffon scarf or shawl.

11–13. *Needle-Art,* 1926. Bows have appeared in fashion and needlecraft magazines as indispensable trimmings for household linens and children's clothing. These bows were designed for beading but could be worked in satin or outline stitches, braiding, needlepoint, even appliqué using real ribbon.

Design Plate, page 41.

14. *Peterson's,* 1863. Originally an embroidery pattern for insertion, work this wheat design in satin stitch and French knots on a skirt, pocket, or cuff.

15. *Peterson's,* 1859. This strikingly modern design was long ago intended for a chemise yoke. Satin stitches and outline embroidery are suitable.

16. *Peterson's,* 1890. A design for embroidery on flannel or cashmere, this design is ideal for eyelet or simple satin stitch embroidery. Or, appliqué the larger shape and add details in embroidery or beading. The elements of the design may be used separately or together, in clusters or rows.

17. *Peterson's,* 1859. A design for silk embroidery on muslin or flannel, this delicate floral band would be lovely in pale shades and fine stitches in floss or crewel wools. Use the design on a belt or strap or along the edges of a jacket.

Design Plate, page 42.

18. *Butterick Designs,* 1910. This band was designed for satin stitch, long and short, and outline embroidery. White, yellow, or pink and two greens were the colors suggested for work on silk, satin, or chiffon. It can be delicate or dramatic, depending on the yarns and colors chosen.

19. *Needle-Craft,* 1890. This floral band first appeared as a border for a Victorian table scarf characteristic of a time when "the prevailing fashion of decorating fancy tables with scarves (was) conducive to charming effects, which do not demand a large outlay of money, provided time and taste can be expended freely." Try this design in outline and satin stitch embroidery on the yokes of a denim skirt and blouse ensemble as illustrated on page 30.

20. *Peterson's,* 1876. Outstanding for its elegant simplicity, this especially beautiful petticoat border was designed for eyelet embroidery. Use buttonhole, satin, or outline stitch. Circles may be eyelets or padded satin stitch. Keep the interpretation light and delicate by using floss or fine crewel wool. Our interpretation on lightweight linen appears on page 26.

Design Plate, page 43.

21, 22. *Peterson's,* 1881. This pattern for a lady's slipper was given full size. Number 21 was the side of the slipper and number 22, the toe. This design has many adaptations for clothing: on a vest, as a central motif on the back of a jacket, on a similarly shaped midriff, on a handbag. Beads or sequins could be substituted for the circular elements of the design.

Design Plate, page 44.

23, 25. *Peterson's,* 1857. These floral embroideries were presented for "young ladies, especially in the country, who have leisure on their hands". The embroidery was to be worked in wool yarn on net and used as an appliqué, to move from one ball gown to another. Work the designs as embroidered appliqués as originally intended, or try them as permanent embroidery or in needlepoint.

24. *The Delineator,* 1892. Described as appropriate for draperies and "an exquisite decoration for party and ball gowns," this flower was designed for a technique known as "fish tail" embroidery in which narrow braid is used to outline the flower and stems. The braid is turned at corners whenever possible and closely stitched in place. The flower petals are worked in a herringbone effect, the centers in a tight cluster of French knots.

Design Plate, page 45.

26. *Butterick Transfers,* 1908. These beautiful Art Nouveau butterflies could grace the back of a linen jacket or find their way to a pillow top as once intended. Use only one of them on a pocket or collar in beading or satin stitch embroidery. Another effective interpretation would be white embroidery on a soft, white cotton or wool challis. Enlarge the design to use for appliqué with embroidered details.

Design Plate, page 46.

27–29. *Vogue Pattern,* 1924. These designs were available as transfer patterns for embroidery. The bold shapes are suitable for pearl cotton or crewel embroidery. Appliqué with embroidered details would be a suitable technique, too, or place mica mirrors in the circles and hold in place with the blanket stitch.

Design Plate, page 47.

30. *Butterick Designs,* 1910. Vivid Oriental shades in pomegranate red, emerald green, and bright orange with black outline accents were suggested for this embroidery design for waists, coats, and skirts. Enlarged, the design is suitable for appliqué with embroidery. It can also be easily adapted to corners for scarves and jackets.

31. *Peterson's,* 1877. A complex braiding pattern for a baby's cloak, this would be easier to work in satin stitch embroidery or quilting. Appliqué and beading are also possible but certainly more difficult.

32. *Needle-Art,* 1920. A typical beading pattern of the period, this design is also appropriate for embroidery. It would be especially lovely on sheer fabrics in either interpretation. Quilting is another possibility.

Design Plate, page 48.

33. *Peterson's,* 1871. Originally a band for embroidery on a petticoat border, this design would be nice on a jacket front or cuffs or as an insert in sleeves. Use fine embroidery thread in simple stitches for a delicate interpretation in white on a pale fabric. For an entirely different look, embroider with bright threads and substitute mica mirrors for the large circular elements in the design.

34. *Godey's,* 1855. This embroidered skirt trimming could be worked in satin stitch or in a combination of braiding and embroidery.

35. *Peterson's,* 1890. This embroidery pattern with its strong geometric shapes could be worked in appliqué with embroidery. In bright colors, it is childlike; in subtle shades or tone on tone, truly sophisticated. In a larger size, the design could be quilted or worked in trapunto.

Design Plate, page 49.

36. *Peterson's,* 1882. This design was intended for a table-cover embroidered in soft shades of silk or linen. It would be lovely on a sweater or jacket, or as an embroidery on a cuff, band, or yoke.

37. *Peterson's,* 1872. It is hard to believe that this elegant design is over 100 years old! It was presented as a needlework design for a baby's mantle. Simple satin stitch embroidery in silk floss or crewel yarn is appropriate as illustrated on page 27. Beading would be an especially beautiful addition.

Design Plate, page 50.

38. *Butterick Transfers* 1926. Neckline embroidery designs were popular for the simple, tubular-shaped fashions of the day. This one was for beads, French knots, buttonhole, outline, or straight stitch embroidery. Work it on the front of a T-shirt in cotton embroidery floss. Use the floral sprays on collars, cuffs, or pockets.

Design Plate, page 51.

39–42. *Butterick Transfers,* 1910. These charming motifs were designed for stenciling, satin stitch, or outline embroidery. Numbers 40 and 42 were originally suggested for buttons. Number 40 is shown in color on page 32. The embroidery was done in embroidery floss on colorful chintz. Use self-cover button forms found in most notions departments, or have the buttons covered professionally.

43, 44. *Needle-Art,* 1924. These two motifs were included as part of a set of stamping patterns with a Mah-Jong theme. The designs are suitable for embroidery or may be enlarged for appliqué. Try either on a pocket, handbag, or jacket.

45. *Godey's,* 1876. Victorian infatuation with paisley and cashmere shawls probably inspired the use of this paisley or "cone" design on a cashmere tablecloth. The cone was appliquéd to a red ground then embellished and surrounded by fancy embroidery stitches in shades of blue and brown. Work this timeless motif in embroidery, beading, braiding, appliqué, or any combination of these techniques.

46. *Peterson's* 1863. Adapted from a red and white embroidered and appliquéd anti-macassar, this floral spray fits comfortably into corners or down the front of a cardigan jacket. Our sample worked in a bright, crewel embroidery on velveteen appears on the cover of this book. The stitches used include satin stitch, long and short, and outline.

Design Plate, page 52.

47. *Butterick Designs,* 1910. These two neckline designs were suggested for satin stitch, eyelet, and outline embroidery on fine fabrics for blouses and children's dresses. Use lazy daisy, French knots, and outline stitches for a quick, contemporary interpretation or try beading on an evening dress.

Design Plate, page 53.

48, 49. *Godey's,* 1834.
50, 51. *Godey's,* 1831.
These delicate motifs for eyelet embroidery can be worked in a combination of stitches: lazy daisy, stem, satin, outline, French knot, and padded eyelet.

1

2

38

6

7

8

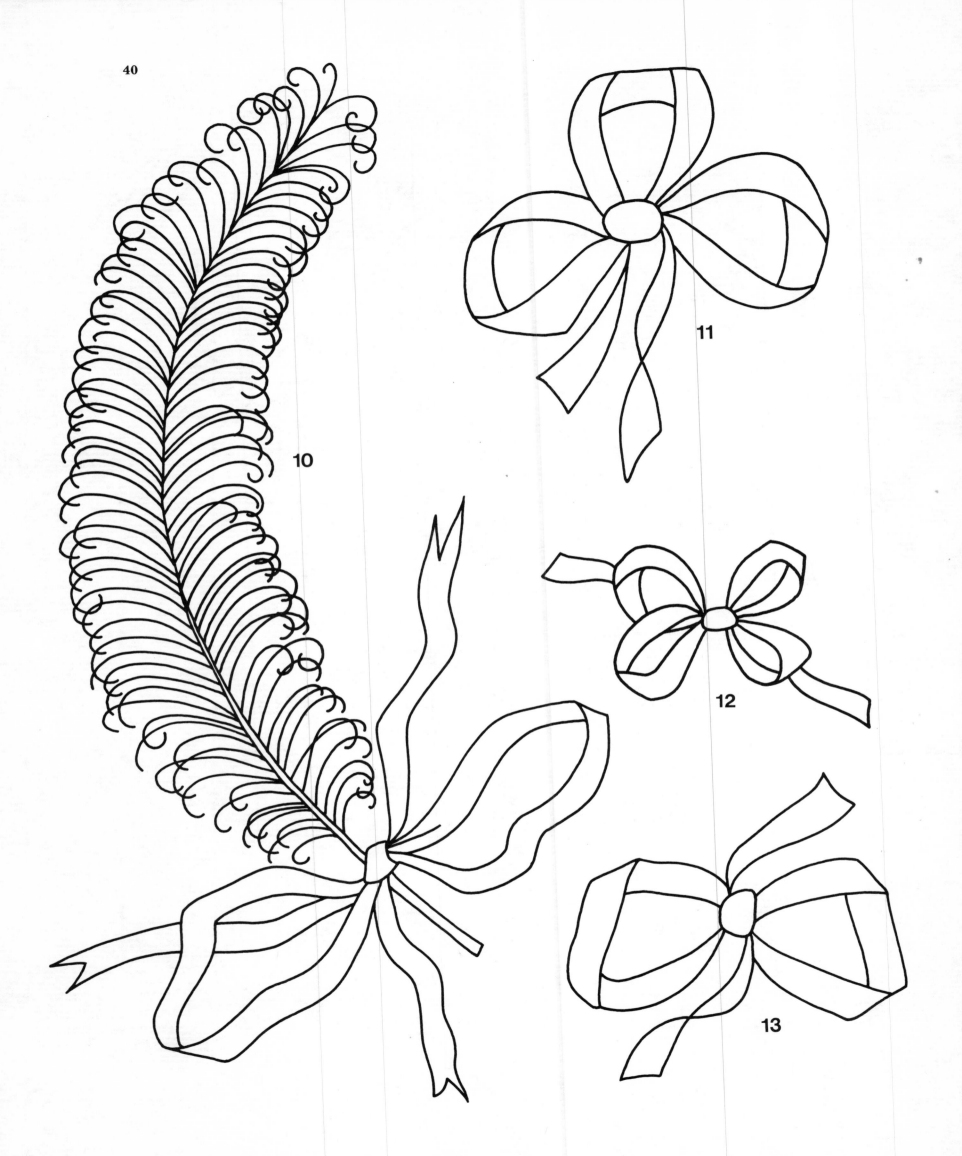

40

10

11

12

13

14

15

16

17

42

18

19

20

44

23

24

25

26

30

31

32

48

33

34

35

36

37

49

38

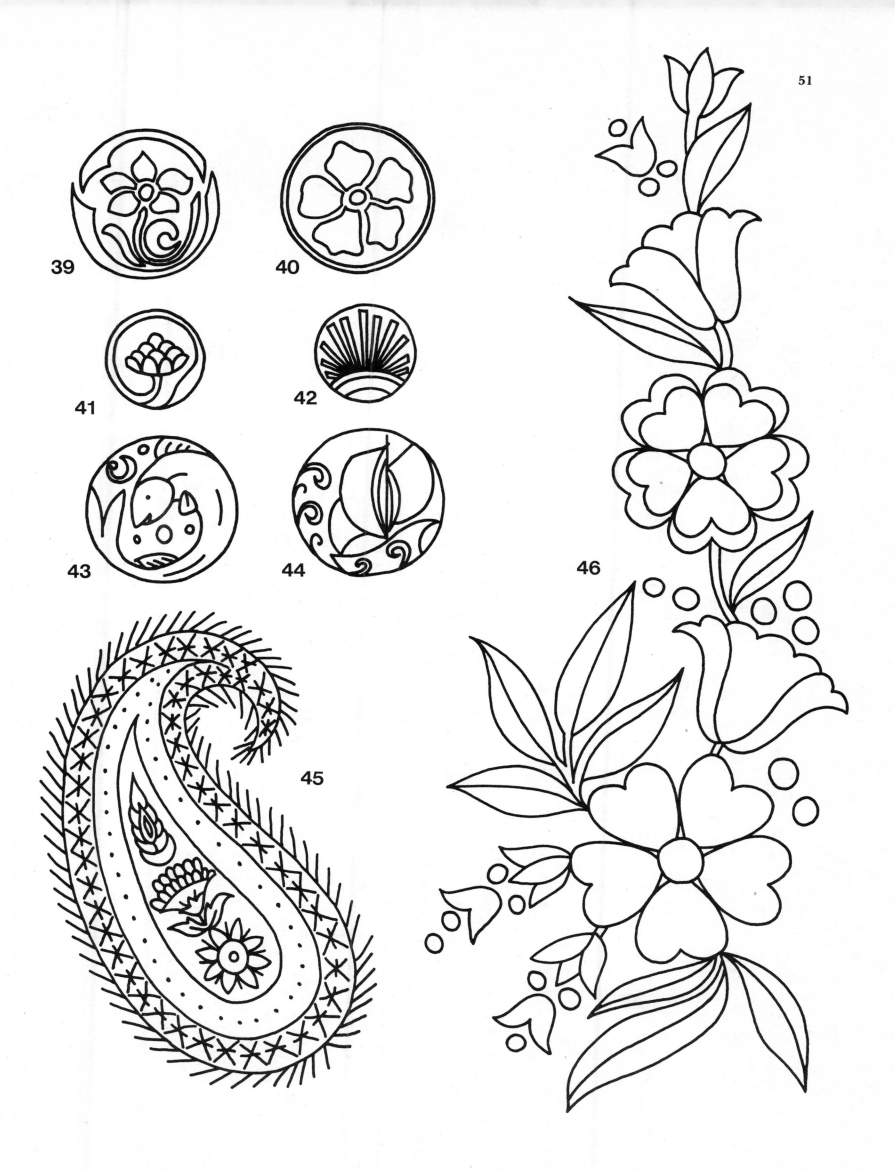

39

40

41

42

43

44

45

46

51

47

48

49

53

50

51

PUNCH-WORK

From 1910 to 1920, punch-work, a lacy, feminine form of counted thread work, was in vogue. In a 1911 article, the editors of *Butterick Designs* wrote that "Punch-work cannot go back and claim a pedigree from ancient embroideries, as many of our recent revivals in stitchery do. It must stand on its own merits as something quite new—but stand it surely will, for it is charming work."

Punch-work is worked with a large, three-sided needle on a lightweight, gauzy fabric. Evenly spaced holes are punched in the fabric and then held in place with an elaborate system of stitches. The area surrounding the work is usually embroidered in delicate floral motifs. Punch-work may also be used to surround an embroidered area as a background. White on white was the traditional color choice for this work, sometimes referred to as "Rhodus" embroidery, but when it is worked with thread in a contrasting color, a smocked effect results. Embroidered French knots can be substituted for the punch stitch for a very different look.

Design Plate, page 55.

52, 53. *Butterick Transfers,* 1913. Work the punched areas first, then use satin stitch to fill in leaves and flowers. Try soft, pastel colors in cotton or silk floss for the embroidery for added interest.

Design Plate, page 56.

54–56. *Butterick Designs,* 1911. The elements of this design were carefully placed and worked on a cotton gauze ruffled shawl as pictured in color on page 20. Outline and satin stitch embroidery in white and off-white pearl cotton surround the delicate punch-work for an especially beautiful effect. Work the design on a purchased shawl or make your own using a commerical pattern.

Design Plate, page 57.

57, 58. *Butterick Designs,* 1912. In this design which is worn by the historical figure on page 20, the morning glory motif surrounds a punch-worked area. Work pastel colored embroidery floss in outline, satin, and blanket stitches for a delicate interpretation.

57

58

BEADING

Beading's long history goes back to primitive man who decorated his clothing with shells, seeds, or bits of bone. Along the way, beads have been legal tender and were favorite items for trade by explorers.

During the 1850's, *Godey's* ran a series, "Bead and Bugle Work," which gave careful instructions for beaded flowers, fringe, buttons, collars, trims, tassels, and ornaments. Then, as now, handworked beaded items represented a substantial savings of money, if not time. The fashion magazine of the last century regularly contained patterns for beaded pen-wipers, table mats, slippers, and handbags, to mention a few. Jet and steel beads were fashionable on clothing in the 1890's; bugle, seed beads, and pearls were popular during the early decades of the twentieth century. Today, beads are used primarily on clothing and appear on everything from T-shirts and tennis shoes to evening wear. They are unsurpassed for imparting richness and elegance to an evening garment.

Linear quilting and braiding designs can serve as a basis for creating beaded edgings, borders, and bands. Most embroidery and appliqué designs with bold uncomplicated shapes can be used for linear or solid beading. Beads can be combined with embroidery, needlepoint, appliqué, or braiding. Beaded designs must be interpreted boldly enough to show from a distance but with enough detail to be interesting up close. Beads should be compatible with their background fabrics and yarns. For instance, try wooden beads with crewel yarns and pearl cotton, delicate beads and spangles with floss.

Design Plate, page 59.

59–61. *Needle-Art,* 1925. These lovely designs were ele-
ments of a stamping pattern for beading. Work the designs in beads or experiment with appliqué and embroidery for an entirely different feeling. Select one motif and quilt it on a jacket or shirt, or combine quilting and braiding and work the band (number 61) along a skirt hem.

Design Plate, page 60.

62–64. *Butterick Transfers,* 1911. Although this design was intended for satin stitch and outline embroidery, it is also easily worked in beading as illustrated on page 31. A combination of beading and silk floss embroidery would also be nice.

Design Plate, page 61.

65. *Vogue Needlework Design,* 1924. Planned for the neckline of a blouse, the suggested techniques for this design were beading and French knot embroidery to create a very elegant garment. The design could also be worked in outline and satin stitch embroidery.

Design Plate, page 62.

66–70. *Butterick Transfers,* 1919. This popular plume motif was available in one pattern and in several versions. It is illustrated in shadow appliqué on a sheer scarf and in braiding on page 23. Although originally intended for beading, it could be interpreted in embroidery and quilting as well.

59

59

60

61

65

62

66

67

68

69

70

BRAIDING

Braiding was a widely accepted method for decorating inexpensive or plain fabric during the nineteenth and early twentieth centuries. One reason for its popularity was that the work went fairly quickly and did not require the consummate skill of embroidery; almost anyone could create a lovely effect with braiding. Designs suitable for braiding were plentiful in *Peterson's, Godey's,* and *Butterick Designs.* Then, as now, the imaginative needleworker could also interpret these same designs in beading, quilting, or embroidery.

Design Plate, page 64.

71. *Butterick Designs,* 1919. *Butterick Designs* featured many segmented motifs for banding like this one based on a circle within a square. It is well suited to a variety of needlework techniques, among them satin stitch embroidery, appliqué, needlepoint, quilting, and trapunto. In our adaptation as it appears on page 32, fake suede was used to create an appliquéd pocket for a tote bag perfect for carry-along needlework projects. Try it in real suede, too.

To make a bag like the one shown, you will need ¾ yard fabric for bag, ½ yard for pocket, and ¼ yard of each color for appliqués. You will also need 1⅛ yards of 27″ stiff interfacing fabric and ½ yard lining fabric. All seam allowances are ½″ wide.

Cut two 12″ squares for pocket. Center and thread trace design on one square. Complete appliqué in chosen method. Remove thread tracing. With right sides together, stitch remaining square to pocket leaving a 6″ opening. Trim seam to ¼″, clip corners, turn and press. Finish opening with slipstitching.

Cut two 16″ × 18½″ rectangles from bag fabric and interfacing. Stitch interfacing to wrong side of each bag section at ⅜″ and trim interfacing close to stitching. Cut two 14″ × 16″ rectangles from lining fabric. With right sides together, stitch each lining section to a bag section across one short end. Trim seams to ¼″ and press open. With right sides facing, stitch bag/lining sections together leaving a 6″ opening in the short end of the lining section. Trim seams, clip corners, and turn through opening in lining. Press edges flat all around, then push lining into bag. Topstitch around open edge of bag at ¼″. Center pocket on one side of bag and baste in place. Slipstitch securely to bag.

For straps, cut two strips of bag fabric 4″ × 31″. Fold each strip in half lengthwise right sides together and stitch across ends and down long edge leaving a 3″ opening. Trim seams, clip corners, turn and press. Slipstitch openings. Topstitch each strap ¼″ from all edges. Position straps on bag 2″ from each side seam with ends extending onto bag 2″ from top edge of bag. Stitch securely in place following lines of topstitching and across top ¼″ from edge of bag.

72. *Needle-Art,* 1920. Braiding, beading, quilting, and embroidery are all appropriate techniques for this medallion. The square shape makes it especially suited for pockets, tote bags, even a pillow.

73. *Butterick Transfers,* 1916. This braiding design would be especially effective used in rows for an all over quilting pattern.

Design Plate, page 65.

74. *Butterick Transfers,* 1916. Silver metallic cording was used to interpret this design on a burgundy shantung evening dress shown on page 25. Outline embroidery, beading, or a combination of appliqué and embroidery are also suitable for this design.

75. *Godey's* 1859. This bold design, originally given as a "braiding pattern for a mantle" is illustrated on page 21 in a combination of braiding and chain stitch embroidery. It is also well-suited for quilting.

Design Plate, page 66.

76. *Peterson's,* 1877. Choose a narrow, flexible braid to interpret this braiding design. Chain stitch embroidery would also be effective.

77. *Needle-Craft,* 1890. This strong design was adapted for braiding from a "Russian Lace" pattern in which the design was outlined in flexible "lace braid" connected with delicate embroidery stitches. Satin stitch embroidery is also a good choice for a contemporary interpretation.

78, 79. *Vogue Needlework Design,* 1924. This complex braided scroll was available as a transfer pattern and makes a particularly effective trim for a soft fabric belt as shown in color on page 32.

Design Plate, page 67.

80–82. *Butterick Designs,* 1910. Try this simple but elegant design in boldly colored satin stitch embroidery or in beading around the neckline of a simple blouse or dress.

64

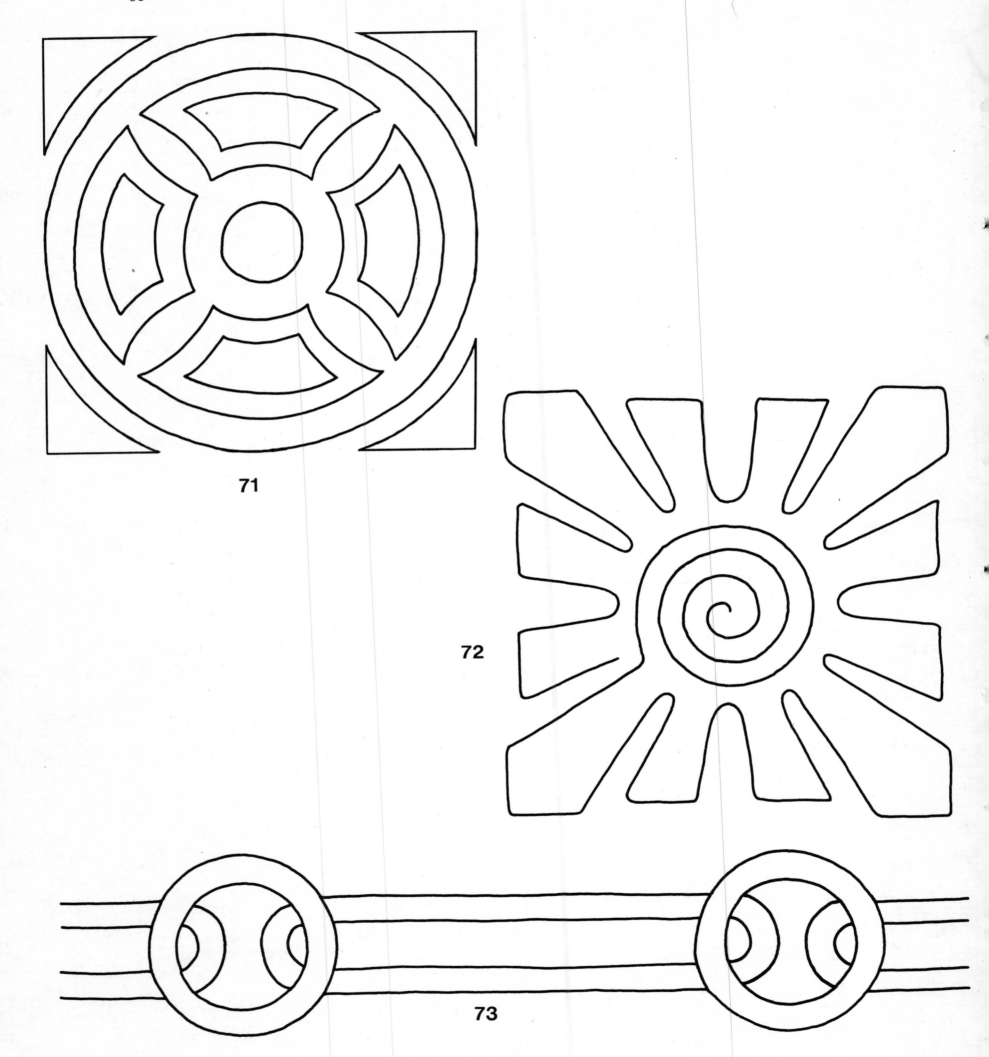

71

72

73

65

74

75

80

81

82

QUILTING

Quilting has long been used for warmth and surface interest in garments and bed coverings. Quilted linings were often found in coats, capes, and robes; petticoats were quilted, too. A skirt which *Godey's* called "the latest thing" in 1863 had a wide band of diamond-shaped quilting around the hem. Historically, quilting was also used to pad clothing into some of fashion's more unusual shapes and under armor for protection from the metal.

Quilting may be done around a printed, patched, or appliquéd design, or it may be an all over, independent pattern or motif of its own. Many linear designs for braiding and beading are also suitable for quilting. Quilting may cover a fabric completely (all over quilting) or it may simply provide ornamentation in specific areas of the fabric or completed garment. Quilting combines well with embroidery, beading, and appliqué.

Trapunto is a form of quilting in which only the design area is padded. Designs for trapunto must have enclosed shapes which can be stuffed to create surface dimension.

Design Plate, page 69.

83. *Butterick Designs,* 1910. This design was included with a set of motifs for beading, braiding, or chain stitch embroidery, techniques for which it is still well-suited. The design is also suited for trapunto as illustrated in our color rendition on page 19.

84. *Butterick Needlework,* 1893. This medallion originated as the principal motif in a fan worked in Rococo embroidery, a type of cut-work, during the reign of Louis XVI (the last half of the 18th century.) Accompanied by a romantic history in which the fan's originator was involved in the French Revolution, *Butterick Needlework* presented the fan and detailed instructions for duplicating it. It is a lovely design for trapunto, satin stitch embroidery, or appliqué.

85. *Peterson's,* 1891. A design for the crown of a smoking-cap (in braid) or a "doyly" (in outline stitch), this design can be worked in quilting, trapunto, or appliqué. Our version is worked in trapunto on a bright yellow satin handbag shown on page 32. It is stitched in buttonhole twist on polyester satin with a crisp underlining backing. Stuffing is polyester fiberfill. A catchstitch channel in buttonhole twist carries the self-cording drawstrings.

Design Plate, page 70.

86. *Needle-Art,* 1923. This design was suggested for beading on a formal gown. It is also suitable for quilting or appliqué with embroidered details. Use a single motif, or, as shown on the design plate, work the design as a band, perhaps on a skirt or sleeve.

87. *Godey's,* 1863. Originally given as a braiding pattern, this design is especially suitable for quilting. For all over quilting, tuck in a repeat of the design, upside down. Outline or solidly bead selected areas for a belt, handbag, or yoke. It would be especially striking in boldly colored patchwork as well.

88. *Needle-Art,* 1926. This graceful, wave-like design originated for braiding, but like so many linear designs it is equally as beautiful when used for quilting. Our version illustrated on page 22 utilizes the design in graduated sizes for all over quilting on a satin jacket.

Design Plate, page 71.

89. *Needle-Art,* 1927. This pillow design appeared under a headline "The old art of quilting brought up to date" during the Twenties revival of patchwork and quilting. The design is perfect for a quilted pocket or tote. Another possibility is solid satin stitch embroidery in bright colors.

69

83

84

85

89

APPLIQUÉ

Appliqué may have originated as a clever method for patching clothing, but eventually it was used for its own merits as a fairly quick method for decorating fabric with bold motifs. The elaborate, self-fabric ruches and ruffles on skirts of the 1830's and 1840's were considered appliqués. Appliqué was often used on quilt tops. Later, petticoats and skirts sported borders in contrasting fabrics, more like appliqué as we know it. Personal accessories such as cigar cases and pocket books as well as items for the home became popular grounds for decorative appliqué.

Today, appliqué is popular as a durable form of decoration for clothing, especially when done by machine. It is ideal for mending, reinforcing, and decorating children's clothing. It is also an effective means of using leftover scraps of fabric.

Appliqué designs must have definite shapes which should be large enough to handle. A design like a flower can be simply cut in one shape or into several different pieces representing petals and leaves. Geometric shapes require precise handling to preserve their geometry. Designs for reverse appliqué should be segmented or have shapes within shapes. Appliqué designs usually can be interpreted in other needlework forms such as embroidery, beading, needlepoint, braiding, quilting, and trapunto. Appliqué itself can be enhanced with most of those techniques and it is possible to construct appliqués of needlepoint, beading, braiding, and embroidery.

Design Plate, page 73.

90. *Butterick Designs,* 1910. Combine appliqué and embroidery for a contemporary interpretation of this Art Nouveau design. Quilt it with buttonhole twist in repeats as a stunning border on the hem of an evening skirt.

Design Plate, page 74.

91. *Butterick Designs,* 1919. This design for ladies' waists and skirts and children's dresses was suggested for satin stitch, outline, seed stitch embroidery, or stenciling. Interpret it today in appliqué, reverse appliqué, or heavy yarn embroidery with a mica mirror for the circle.

92. *Needle-Art,* 1920. This was one of the most enduring designs in the Butterick collection and was suggested as a motif or banding for embroidery. It makes a charming appliqué with straight stitch and French knot accents.

93. *Peterson's,* 1889. This design was presented in *Peterson's* on a colored plate and originated in the fifteenth century! It was suggested as a border for curtains or a table-cover but, could be used as an all over quilting design or appliqué. To appliqué, use two different colors for the leaves; appliqué or embroider each cloverleaf.

Design Plate, page 75.

94. *Butterick Designs,* 1910. This simplistic flower was intended for stenciling, a popular craft of the early 1900's. Try embroidery, appliqué, or reverse appliqué.

95. *Peterson's,* 1881. This poppy for a tea-cloth was intended for crewel embroidery worked in long and short and outline stitches. For appliqué, cut the flower as one, the leaves separately, and embroider the veining and petal lines. Appliqué or embroider the flower center.

96. *Peterson's,* 1877. A flower planned for use on "those appliquéd table-covers now so fashionable," *Peterson's* suggested buttonhole stitch for the edges in colored silk. Along the leaf and petal veins and the stamens use an outline stitch; finish each stamen with a French knot.

Design Plate, page 76.

97, 98. *Butterick Designs,* 1919. Center this medallion on a simple T-shirt or sweater and work in lightly stuffed trapunto. The simple shapes make this design suitable for appliqué and embroidery as well. Use bias trim for the edges of the design and add details in outline stitch.

Design Plate, page 77.

99, 100. *Butterick Designs,* 1910. These carefully segmented designs, characteristic of the early 1900's, are especially suited to appliqué and to satin stitch embroidery. Oriental shades of color were popular for embroidery when these two designs were available in transfer patterns. Cobalt blue was suggested for the irises.

Design Plate, page 78.

101. *Butterick Designs,* 1910. This design was intended for appliqué or outline embroidery on a pillow or table runner. It could be worked in appliqués of satin on the back of a jacket. Try satin stitch embroidery in two shades of the same color to work the birds.

Design Plate, page 79.

102. *Butterick Designs,* 1912. Imagine this lovely old stenciling pattern on the corner of a sheer scarf or triangular shawl in pastel shades of shadow appliqué. Consider the classic tulip for embroidery, punch-work, quilting, or trapunto.

Design Plate, page 80.

103. *Butterick Designs,* 1910. This design was given for a combination of fabric stenciling and embroidery on scarves, hangings and pillows. It may be worked in appliqué or reverse appliqué.

74

91

92

93

97

98

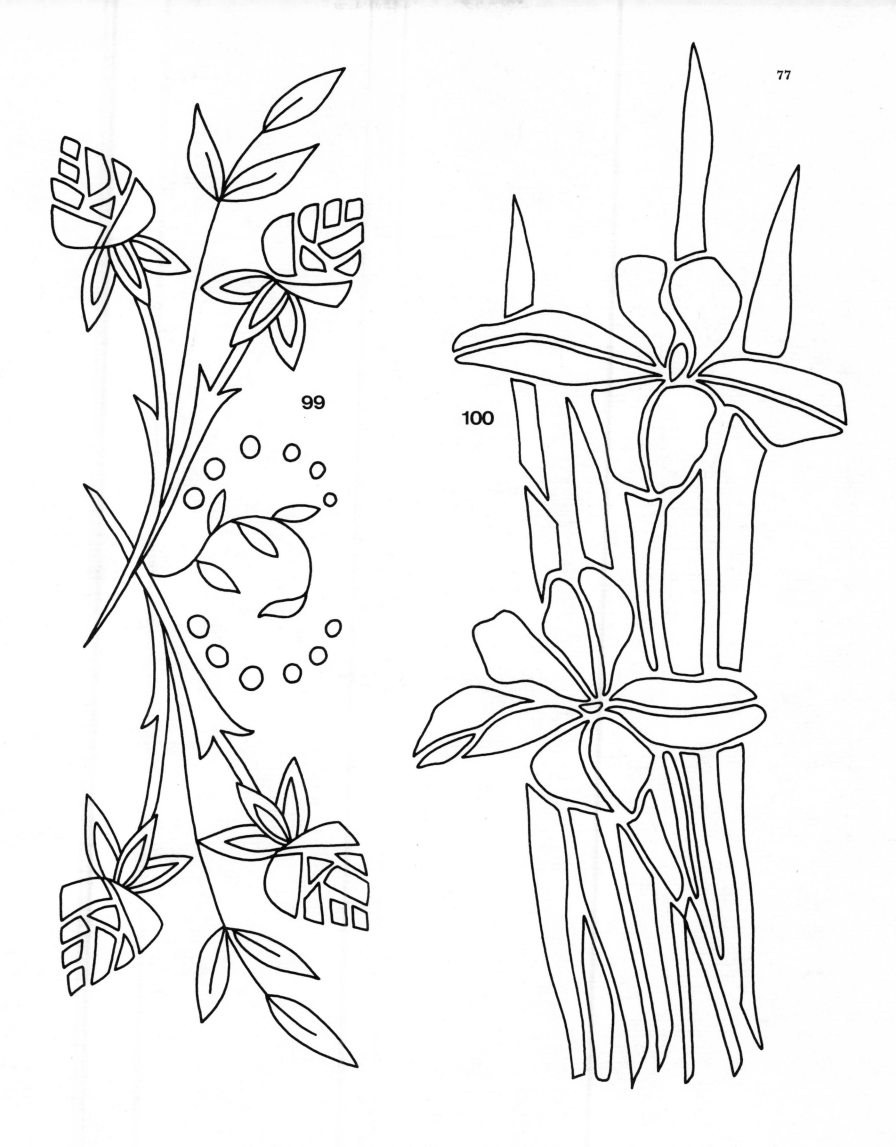

99

100

77

101

102

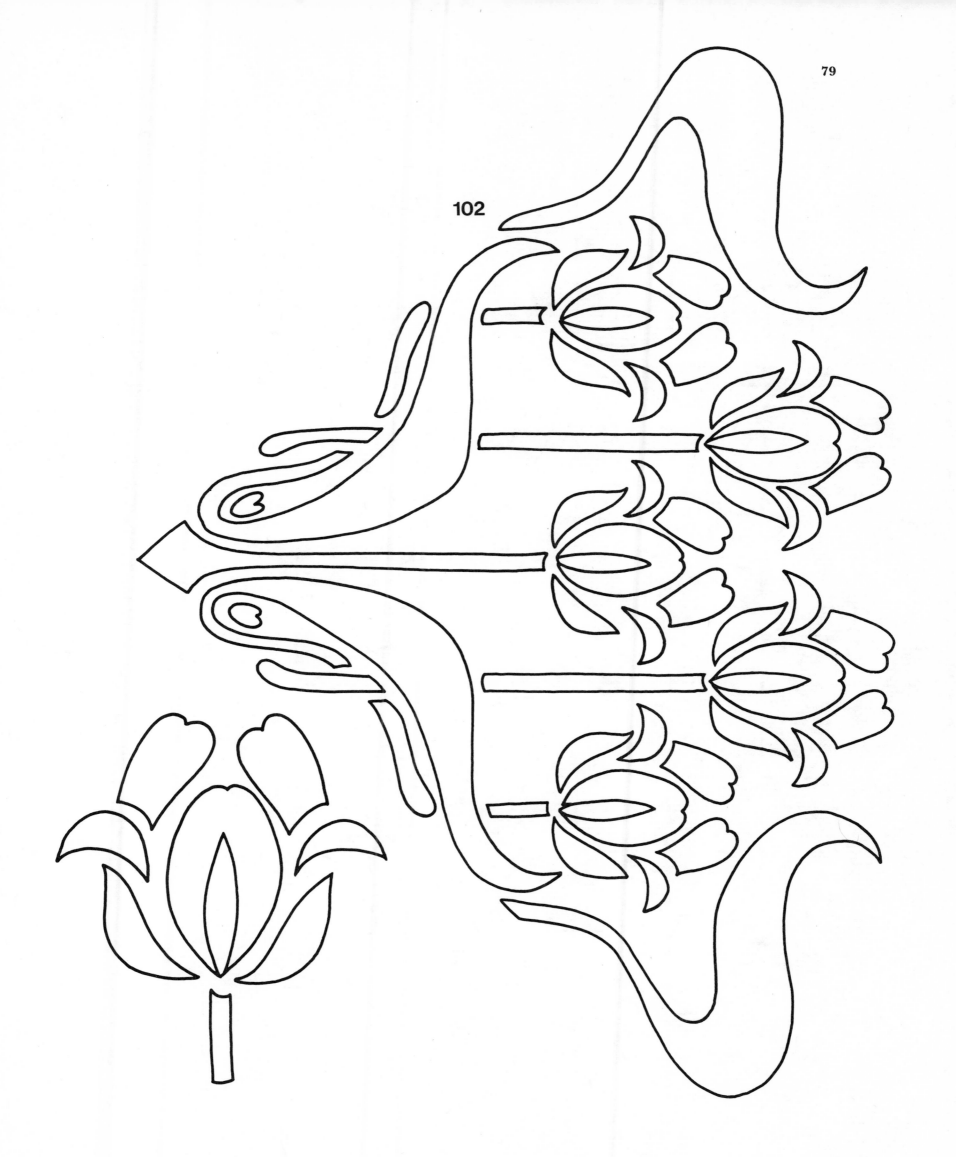

103

PATCHWORK

Prior to the development of the American fabric industry, fabrics were too precious to waste even a single piece. Scraps and worn clothing alike were recycled into pieced and appliquéd patchwork for bedcoverings. Later, patchwork developed as a decorative art, and elaborate combinations of silks, velvets, and fancy embroidery stitches found favor in the anti-macassars, ottomans, tablecovers, and cushions of Victorian parlors.

Patchwork experienced periodic revivals then, as now. The fact that it is a uniquely American craft and that it is a successful method for recycling fabrics, has contributed largely to its current favor. Patchwork is being used in all manner of clothing and personal and home accessories. And today, American ingenuity has gone one step further and created fabric printed to look like patchwork!

Patchwork designs are a rich source of ideas to work in other needlework forms, notably embroidery and needlepoint. Many of the shapes are suitable for appliqué as well as piecing.

Patchwork for clothing can be handled in a number of different ways. Garments can be cut from patchwork fabric or a series of patchwork blocks can be assembled to the shape of a garment piece. Or, a single patchwork block, or element, or strip of blocks may be appliquéd to already constructed clothing and accessories or used to form actual items such as tote bags, scarves, pockets, bibs, and yokes. Of course, these designs are all suitable for patchwork bed coverings and pillows. Many of them would be stunning translated into hooked rugs.

Design Plate, page 82.

104. *Peterson's,* 1872. Patchwork designs are often suitable for needlepoint and this intriguing design is no exception. It was used in a modified form to decorate the tennis racquet cover shown on page 32. The work was done in three shades of magenta on navy blue with Persian wool but the original instructions for traditional patchwork required as many as six different colors to create a bed quilt or crib-cover.

Design Plate, page 83.

105,106. *Godey's,* 1858. For a time, *Godey's* presented two new patchwork designs like these each month. Usually, no instructions were given leaving much to the imagination and skill of the worker. The first of these two combines scallops, ovals, and stars appliquéd to a plain background. The star may be cut as one piece, or pieced together with eight diamond shapes. The Stars and Bars design would be particularly striking in patriotic colors. Piece the five-pointed star from diamond shapes, then apply to a solid ground. The "bars" are complex and composed of rectangles, parallelograms, triangles, and squares which can also be pieced and then applied to the background fabric. Use these two designs to create patchwork cloth for complete patchwork garments or isolate elements of each for appliqué accents on otherwise plain garments and accessories. Consider them for needlepoint as well.

Design Plate, page 84.

107. *Godey's,* 1858. An unusual floral pattern for appliquéd patchwork. Use it for a bold, peasantlike border on a long gathered skirt.

108. *Godey's,* 1861. *Godey's* needlework editor also suggested that "this design may be . . . worked on (needlepoint) canvas in wools (with) the outlines done in black." Orange, claret, blue, and brilliant greens were the suggested colors.

Design Plate, page 85.

109. *Godey's,* 1859. This complex, undulating piecework design relies on careful placement of color. The work may be entirely pieced or the "chain" may be pieced and then appliquéd to a background fabric. It appears as a band at the hem of a jumper in our version on page 28.

110. *Godey's,* 1859. This chevron pattern is composed of parallelograms in two sizes. Try it in several shades of one color for an ombré effect or in bright rainbow colors. If used to create an all over patchwork garment, treat the completed fabric like a stripe for matching purposes. Needlepoint in bargello would also be an excellent choice of technique.

104

105

106

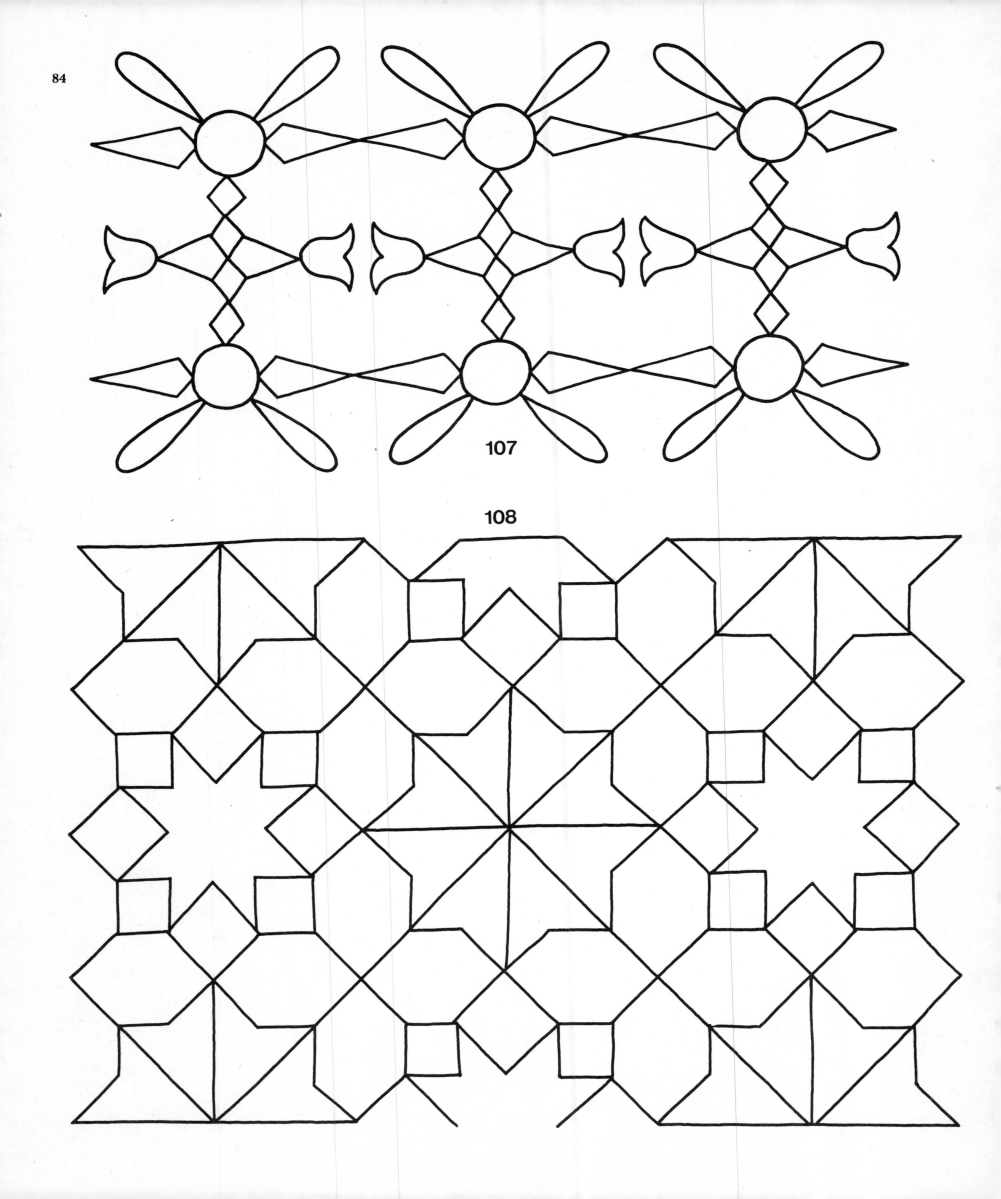

107

108

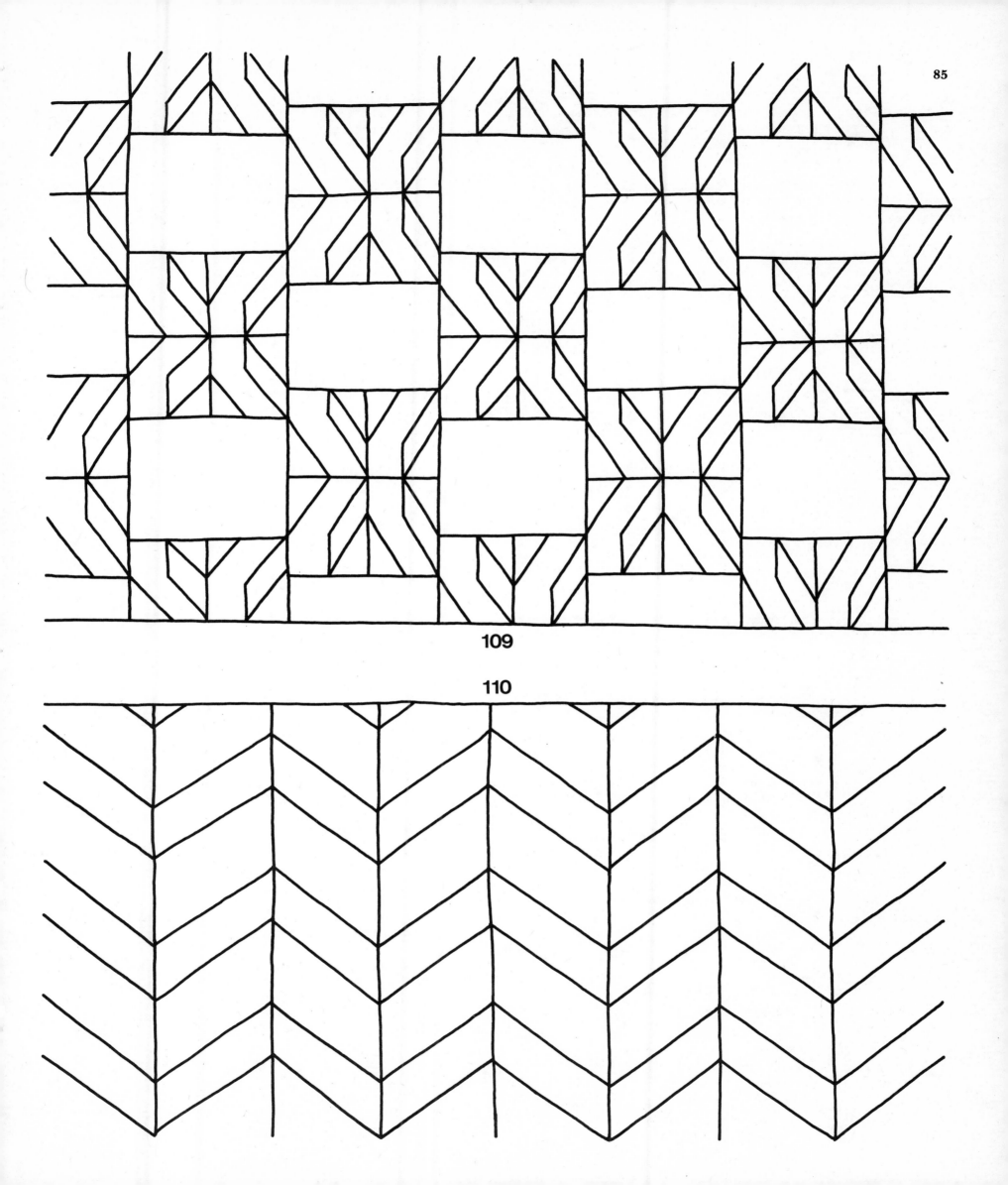

109

110

NEEDLEPOINT

Needlepoint worked on stiff canvas was a development of the 1800's and until recently has been confined to upholstery, rugs, pillows, pictures, and accessories such as slippers, bags, and belts. The fabric created by needlepoint on canvas is fairly stiff but with careful planning and execution, it can be used to form or decorate clothing as well as accessories.

Needlepoint was called Berlin Work in the 1800's because the colorful patterns for this form of counted thread embroidery originated in Berlin. It was a dominant form of needlework in the 19th century. The magazines of the era regularly contained one or two colored graph designs for needlepoint to be done in the spirit of Berlin Work.

Needlepoint patterns can also be interpreted in cross-stitch embroidery and often in filet crochet. Many embroidery, patchwork, and appliqué patterns are suitable for needlepoint, too. Needlepoint can be used to make buttons, handbags, belts, bracelets, neckbands, hatbands, camera and book straps. Needlepoint appliqués make lovely pockets. Needlepoint designs worked in an all over pattern in large pieces can be treated as cloth to form complete garments or garment sections. These special techniques are included in the instruction section at the back of this book.

Design Plate, page 88.

111. *Peterson's,* 1857. These calla lilies first graced the toe and side band of a lady's needlepointed slipper. Accord-ing to the magazine editors, the design was the "handsomest ever published in any magazine, whether abroad or at home." It was given in color as "an extra plate to our subscribers" as a "slight way of showing our thanks for their liberal patronage."

Design Plate, page 89.

112. *Peterson's,* 1889. This design was adapted from one for Berlin Work which appeared in color as a "New Year's Gift" to *Peterson's* subscribers. Cross-stitch is also suitable.

113. *Needle-Art,* 1920. This charming cherub originally appeared as a filet crochet design for a sideboard set. Our contemporary interpretation is for needlepoint or cross-stitch in brightly colored yarns. Work it for a belt, a patch or pocket, an appliqué, or as a special valentine.

Design Plate, page 90.

114. *Peterson's,* 1871. This design from a stripe for an ottoman cushion is given here in the original colors suggested by the *Peterson's* needlework editor. Work the main motif as a belt buckle or for an appliqué on a handbag. It would make a striking pillow. Cross-stitch embroidery is another suitable technique.

115. *Peterson's,* 1857. This pattern for a chair stripe in Berlin Work appeared on a vividly colored plate about

which the magazine boasted, "Nothing so beautiful as this plate has ever appeared, of its kind, in any other American Magazine." Our version as a belt worked with embroidery floss on #14 Penelope canvas in Oriental colors appears on page 32. The symbol is the sign of longevity.

Design Plate, page 91.

116. *Needle-Art,* 1920. The butterfly has long been a popular design motif. This one appeared in an article on fashioning beaded neck chains. Our interpretation on page 32 is in needlepoint on a specially constructed, ready-made luggage tag with a canvas insert. Another suitable interpretation would be beads or sequins for an appliqué on an evening gown or handbag.

117. *Needle-Art,* 1924. This charming sampler appears on the color plate, page 24 in needlepoint and cross-stitch embroidery. It would make an equally lovely pillow or picture, in either technique.

Design Plate, page 92.

118. *The Delineator,* 1902. "A cozy-corner or a couch calls for a number of pillows and they need to be piled up on one another with a studied carelessness inviting to behold." This design for clematis flowers appeared in color for just such a sofa cushion.

The current interpretation appears in color on page 32 as an exceptionally beautiful evening bag. The petit point was worked in a combination of six-strand silk embroidery floss for the flowers and vines and a single strand of Persian yarn for the background. Bugle beads and a bit of embroidery add the finishing touches.

To duplicate the bag, work the design in petit point following the basic needlepoint instructions which begin on page 120. After blocking, machine stitch around the needlepoint close to stitches. Trim away excess canvas to 1/2" on all sides. Measure finished needlepoint area. Cut one piece of satin the width and twice the height of the finished needlepoint plus 1/2" for seam allowances all around. Cut another piece of satin the width and three times the finished height plus 1/2" for seam allowances all around. Cut two pieces of heavyweight, nonwoven interfacing and one piece of polyester fleece the same size as the larger piece of satin. Trim 1" from one long edge of the fleece. Stitch needle-point to bottom third of one interfacing piece very close to needlepoint stitches on all sides. Add bead and embroidered details to worked flowers if desired.

With right sides together, stitch shorter piece of satin to top edge of needlepoint through canvas and interfacing using previous stitching on interfacing as a stitching guide. Press seam away from needlepoint. Place remaining piece of satin over needlepoint/satin section, right sides together. Layer remaining interfacing and fleece over satin. Fleece should not extend into seam allowances along the long sides. Pin together. With needlepoint section on top, stitch all around in a 1/2" seam. In the needlepoint area, use original stitching through interfacing as a stitching guide. Leave a 6" opening on the end opposite the needlepoint. Trim seams and corners. Turn, press, slipstitch opening. Turn one-third of bag up to form pouch and slipstitch edges together securely. Attach Velcro or snap fastener under needlepoint flap.

Design Plate, page 93.

119–121. *Needle-Art,* 1924. These bright little designs once appeared on a graph of "gay cross-stitch for sundry uses" in a spring issue of *Needle-Art.* Try the perky parrot or the flower basket in cross-stitch or duplicate stitch on a sweater or in needlepoint on a pocket or tote bag. The bouquet is just the right size for cross-stitch on a collar or pocket or it could be used in repeats for a pretty border.

Design Plate, page 94.

122. *Godey's,* 1874. This fierce dragon was presented for Berlin Work on a railway bag. Embroider him on a pocket or jacket back or graph the pattern for cross-stitch or needlepoint on a tote or handbag. Strong greens, reds, and oranges on a dark background are good color choices.

Design Plate, page 95.

123. *Peterson's,* 1888. This carnation was adapted from a Berlin Work stripe, another "New-Year's Gift" to *Peterson's* subscribers. The original design appeared as a continuous stripe repeat and was "intended for the back of a chair, to be inserted between two bands of satin, velvet, or plush."

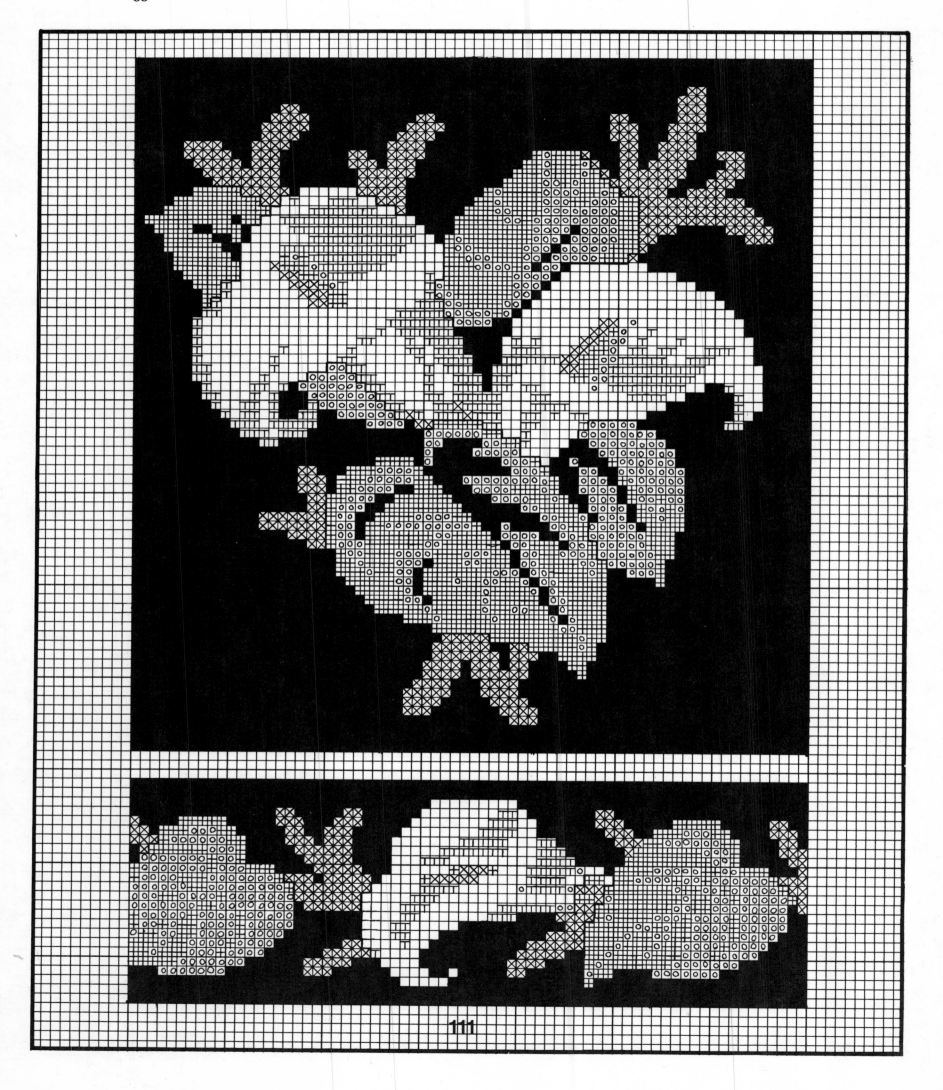

112

113

Scale: 10 stitches per inch. Designs may be worked on any size canvas but size of completed work will change accordingly. For graph color key, see page 122.

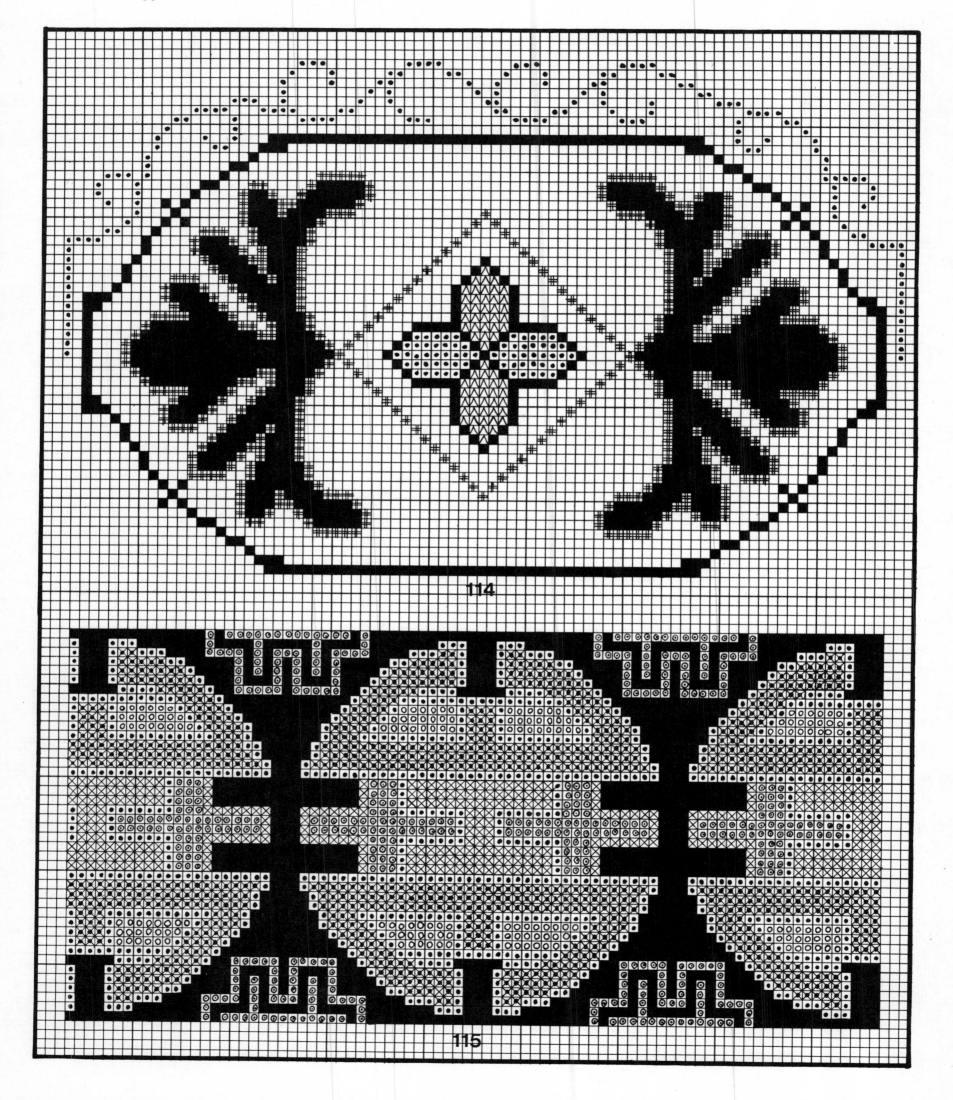

114

115

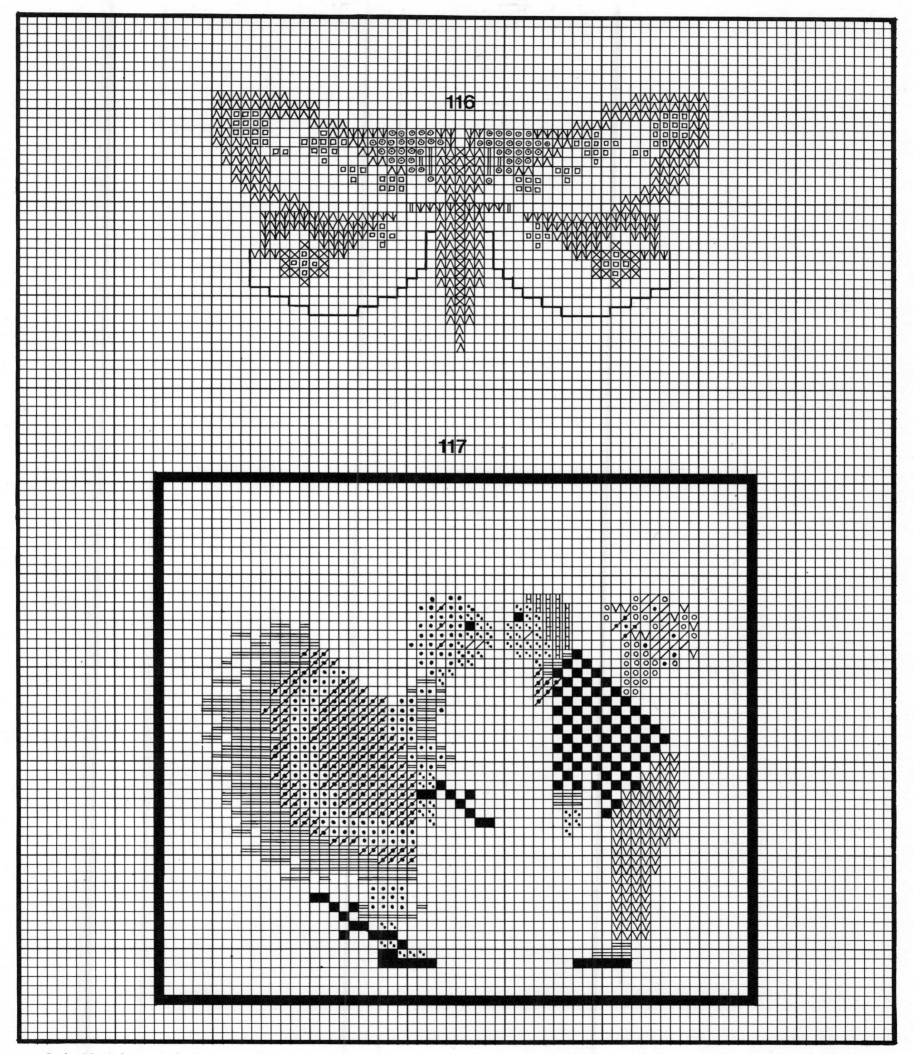

116

117

118

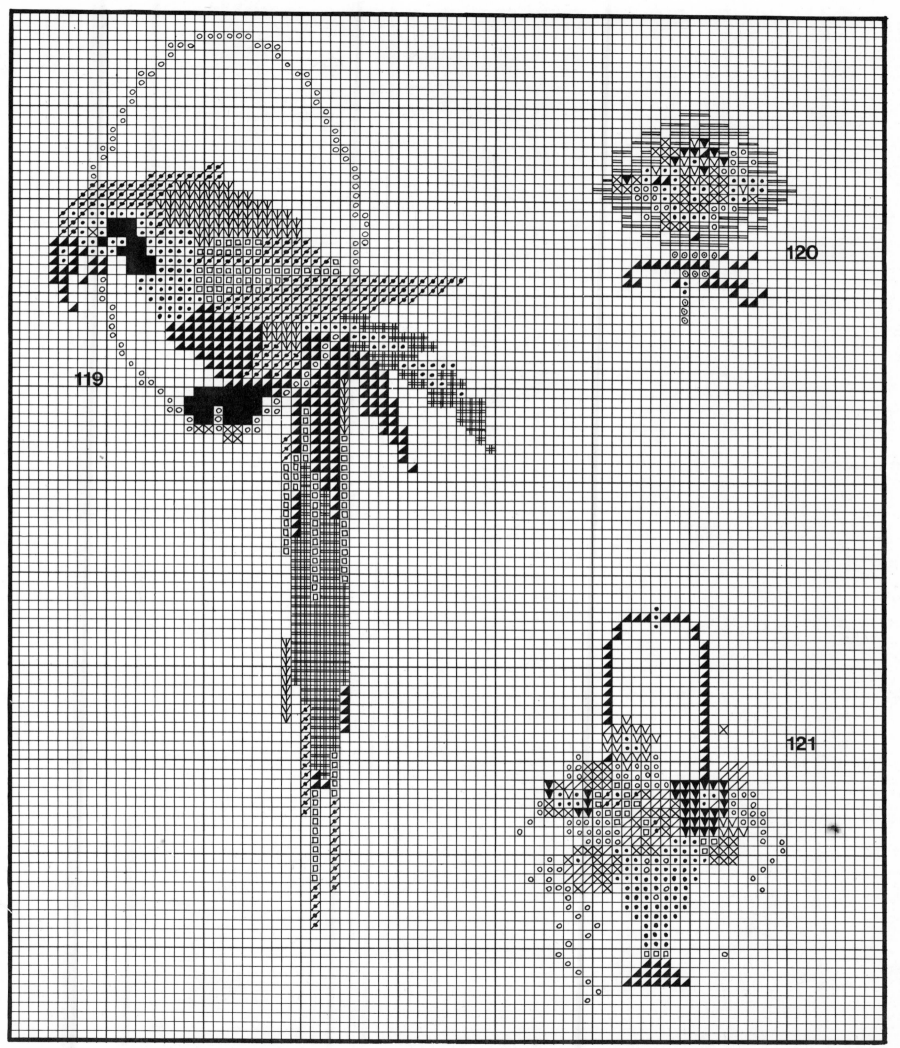

119

120

121

Scale: 10 stitches per inch. Designs may be worked on any size canvas but size of completed work will change accordingly. For graph color key, see page 122.

122

123

FILET CROCHET

Filet crochet, or "square crochet" as it was called in an 1867 article in *Peterson's* became a popular needlework form in the 1860's, inspired by the popularity of Irish lace. It was used extensively in creating "tidies" to protect the backs and arms of chairs from soil and wear.

In the 1920's, filet crochet became so popular for decorating household linens and pillows, that a variation called "filet lace" developed in which one worked the design from a graph in a darning stitch over the blocks of a purchased filet mesh. This technique can be duplicated today with acrylic yarns woven through casement fabric. Filet crochet worked in fine cotton with a fine hook was widely used to trim home-sewn lingerie and sleepwear.

There are many contemporary uses for filet crochet. It may be gathered or left flat for edgings. Strips, blocks, or single motifs may be inserted in or appliquéd to fabrics. During the 1920's, a sheer pastel lining was often placed behind the filet work used for insertions. A strip of filet crochet can become a hat band, a choker necklace, or a tie belt when attached to a strip of matching or contrasting ribbon for stability.

Filet crochet is worked from graphed patterns, many of which are also suitable for needlepoint and cross-stitch embroidery. The filled-in squares on the graph represent solid blocks of crochet; open squares on the graph represent open blocks of the crochet mesh. The color symbols on some of the following designs are for use with cross-stitch or needlepoint interpretations and should be disregarded for crochet.

Design Plate, page 97.

124. *Butterick Transfers,* 1919. This design was originally worked as a filet crochet yoke on a sleeveless nightgown. Create a whimsical, colorful needlepoint or cross-stitch belt from this pattern in red and green yarns on a white ground.

125. *Needle-Art,* 1920. The butterflies which now enhance the blouse pictured on our cover were once intended for use on "dainty underwear." In the cover version, the crocheted bands were used as insertion at the yoke and as appliqués down the front of the blouse.

126. *Needle-Art,* 1920. These roses were intended for a crocheted lace edging on a delicate luncheon set.

127. *Needle-Art,* 1922. This filet crochet band for insertion is just as easily used for a flat lace edging and ruffled collar as shown in color on page 29. Cross-stitch and needlepoint are also suitable.

Design Plate, page 98.

128–130. *Peterson's,* 1874. These lacy designs, reminiscent of snowflakes, were designed for "tidies" for embroidery on Java canvas, a rather stiff basketweave fabric once used for counted thread embroideries. They are especially attractive in brightly colored needlepoint on ready-made accessories like the checkbook holder shown in color on page 32.

131, 133. *The Delineator,* 1893. These cross-stitch borders were recommended for dresses and aprons. During the early 1890's, this work was called "Russian" embroidery due to its imitation of the unique color combinations and designs used on Russian peasant gowns. Needlepoint, as well as filet crochet, is also an appropriate technique for working these designs.

132. *Peterson's,* 1874. Another design originally intended for embroidery on Java canvas, this one would be lovely on a belt or hat band worked in needlepoint.

134, 135. *The Delineator,* 1892. In a special article on "Russian" embroidery (cross-stitch in bright colors), *The Delineator* recommended working these two designs on a checked material as the check provided "an excellent guide for the work." Cross-stitch embroidery on traditional, checked ginghams is still a popular way to avoid the necessity of counting threads to achieve evenly worked embroidery of this type.

Design Plate, page 99.

136. *Peterson's,* 1874. The rose has long been a favorite flower for needlework. This especially lovely motif for filet crochet would make a beautiful needlepointed tote bag for carrying your needlework essentials.

137. *Needle-Art,* 1920. This floral swirl was once intended to enhance the neckline and cuffs of a very feminine blouse. We show it on page 32 worked in needlepoint on a special ready-made billfold.

128

129

131

132

133

134

135

ALPHABETS

Alphabets are essential to monograms, a classic and very personal way to embellish clothing, linens, and personal accessories. In the formal sense, a monogram is a design composed of one's initials, often intertwined, sometimes set in a wreath or within a floral motif. Each month *Godey's* and *Peterson's* offered initials for marking (it often took several issues to collect an entire alphabet) and full names for the same purpose. In these magazines the initial letter of many articles was often an elaborate design and no doubt this provided additional inspiration.

Traditionally, there were formal rules regarding the placement of a monogram on household items but for personal items more latitude was permitted. Placement was a personal matter although *Butterick Designs* cautioned in 1913 that, "In the case of lingerie, eccentricity in placing is especially to be guarded against."

In a formal monogram, the last name initial is given prominence. It is placed last in a horizontal or vertical placement, or centered in a monogram where the central letter is enlarged. When all the letters are the same size, the surname initial comes last.

Today, names, initials, and even words are boldly emblazoned across T-shirts, handbags, and pockets. Many needlework techniques may be used to interpret alphabets. A needlepoint tote shouts "tennis," a child's smock is appliquéd "I like to paint" and "I love you" winds around a belt in braiding or chain stitch embroidery.

Design Plate, page 101.

138. *Butterick Designs,* 1908. This elegant alphabet was chosen to personalize the tie on page 32. The monogram is embroidered in silk floss in satin stitch and French stemming which were traditional stitches for monogramming.

To monogram a ready-made tie, remove the lining from the back and work through the tie fabric only, not through the interfacing. Resew tie when embroidery is completed.

Design Plate, page 102.

139. *Godey's,* 1858. This alphabet for crochet was designed for personalizing anti-macassars and other crocheted items of the era. See it in needlepoint on a tennis racquet cover on page 32.

Design Plate, page 102.

140. *Needle-Art,* 1924. Filet crochet was at a peak during the 1920's and this lovely alphabet was useful for marking table and bed linens. It could also be worked in cross-stitch or needlepoint.

Design Plate, page 104.

141. *Artistic Alphabets,* 1893. This interesting fancy block alphabet is ideal for embroidery in satin stitch or outline stitch filled in with seed stitch or feather stitch. Enlarged, the alphabet can be interpreted in appliqué or trapunto.

Design Plate, page 105.

142. *Vogue Embroidery Design,* 1922. Select the appropriate initials from this monogram set and work it in satin stitch on pockets, scarves, and collars. It would be a lovely addition on a satin clutch bag or lingerie case. Pad stitch the largest letter, the surname initial, for an elegant effect.

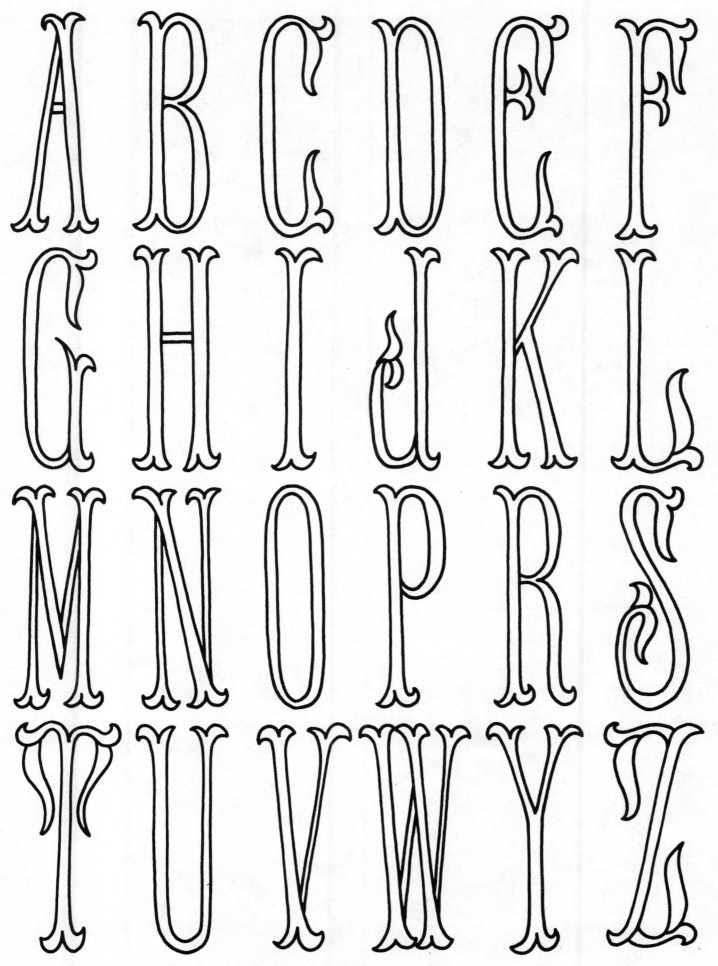

138

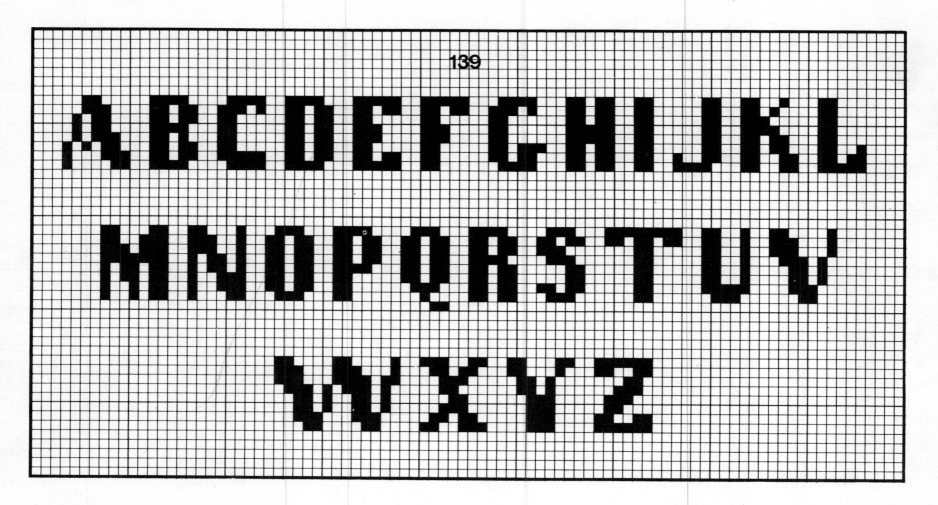

139

ABCDEFGHIJKL
MNOPQRSTUV
WXYZ

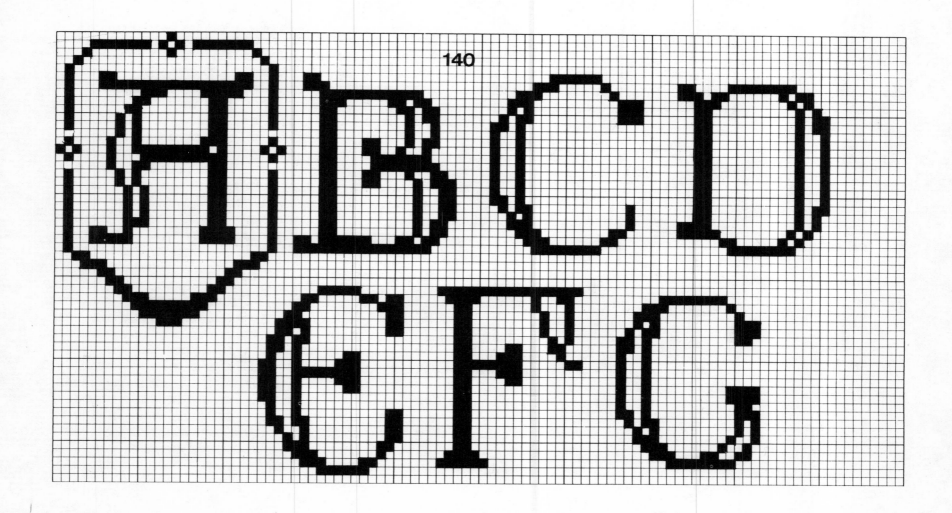

140

ABCD
EFG

140

Scale: 10 stitches per inch. Designs may be worked on any size canvas but size of completed work will change accordingly. For graph color key, see page 122.

ABCDE
FGHIJ
KLMNO
PQRST
UVWX
YZ

105

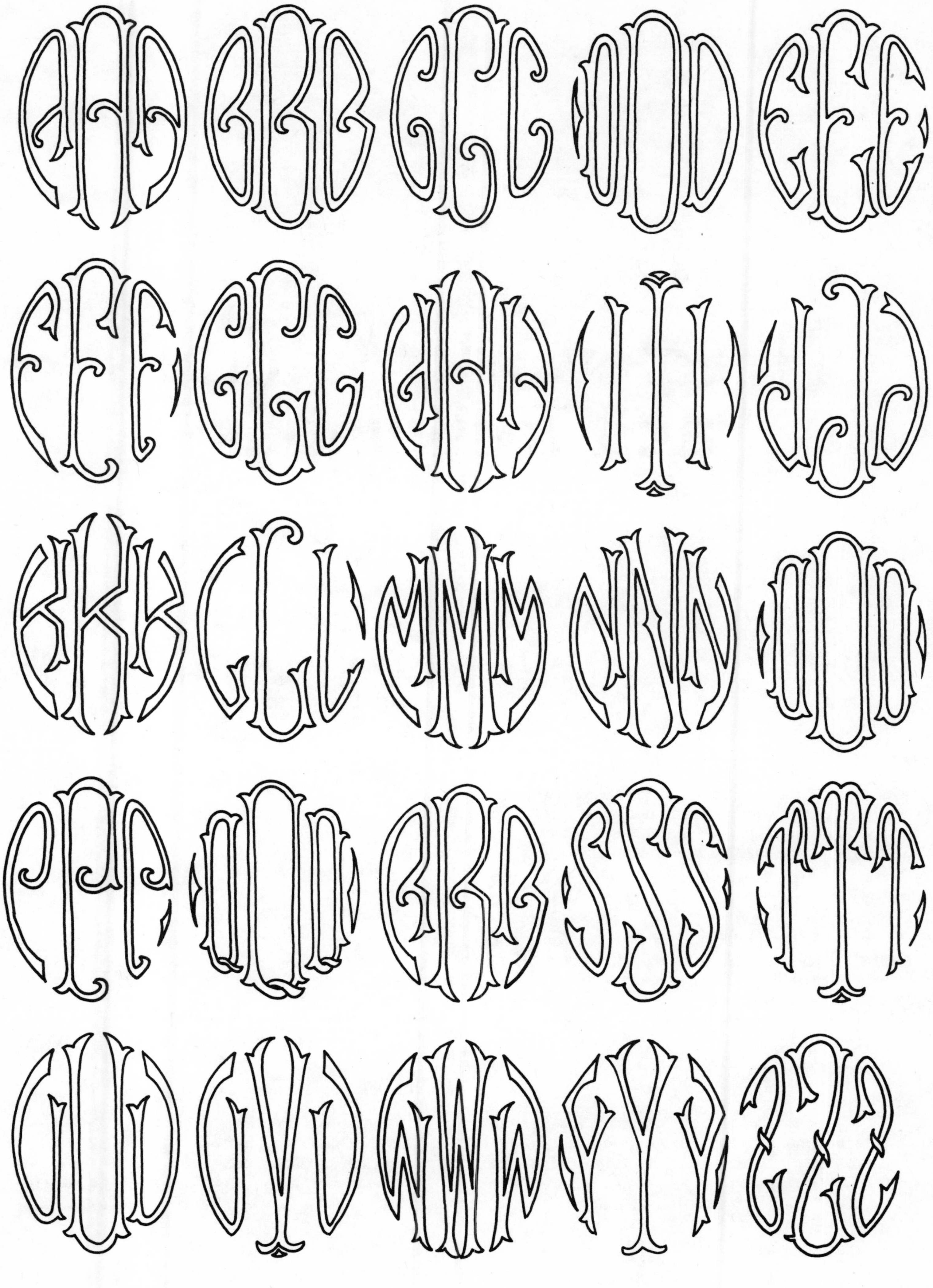

4

Needlework Materials and Techniques

Embroidery

In its very broadest sense, embroidery is the surface decoration of fabric with stitches. The stitches may fill in a design or merely outline it. Hand embroidery styles range from carefully counted cross-stitch to carefree stitches of free-style embroidery. In addition, embroidery stitches are the basis for many other forms of needlework.

Designs may be worked with a variety of stitches and an endless assortment of yarns. The addition of other elements like beads, sequins, and mirrors adds excitement and glamour when combined with embroidery stitches. Embroidery can also be combined with other forms of needlework including appliqué and patchwork.

Materials

Fabric
Many fabrics are suitable for embroidery and the fabric must be coordinated with the weight and texture of the yarn. Smooth, loosely woven fabrics are easier to work. Lightweight fabrics for backing include organdy, voile, organza, batiste, soft or crisp underlinings.

Yarn, Thread
Many types of yarns may be used for embroidery. Some common ones are cotton embroidery floss, matte cotton, pearl cotton, crewel yarn, tapestry yarn.

Needles
Embroidery/crewel needles are slender with a sharp point and a long eye. Tapestry needles have a blunt point and large eye.

Hoops
Hoops are essential for most embroidery because they hold the fabric taut while stitching and help the stitcher control tension. Always buy hoops with an adjustable screw to allow accommodation of a variety of fabrics.

Basic Procedure for Embroidery

1. Prepare and press fabric. Transfer design to fabric.
2. Assemble hoops and fabric. Move hoops from one area to another as work progresses. To protect the completed stitching, tissue paper may be placed between the hoops and stitches. Always remove hoops

at the end of a work session to prevent hard creases from forming in the fabric.

3. Begin embroidery by tying a knot in the end of the yarn and passing the yarn from the right side to the underside of the fabric about ½″ from the starting point on a design line. Take a few embroidery stitches along the design line catching the yarn with each stitch. When you finish each yarn, weave the yarn end into a few stitches on the back of the work. (Knots to begin and end a yarn are usually not recommended because they may untie allowing pulled stitches which ultimately destroy the piece. They may also create lumps in your work.)

4. When embroidery is completed, clean if necessary. Press or block.

5. Complete garment construction or resew ready-made garment, if necessary.

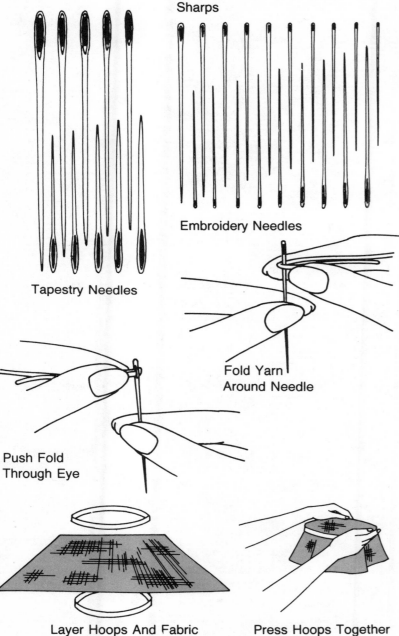

Sharps

Embroidery Needles

Tapestry Needles

Fold Yarn Around Needle

Push Fold Through Eye

Layer Hoops And Fabric

Press Hoops Together

The Stitches

These are some basic embroidery stitches you might use to execute the designs in *Needlework Classics*. There are many more.

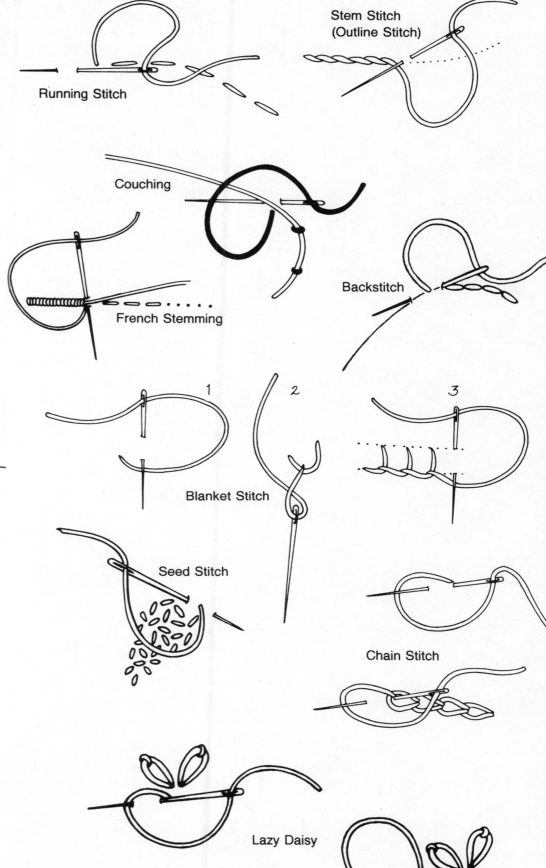

Running Stitch

Stem Stitch (Outline Stitch)

Couching

Backstitch

French Stemming

1   2   3

Blanket Stitch

Seed Stitch

Chain Stitch

Lazy Daisy

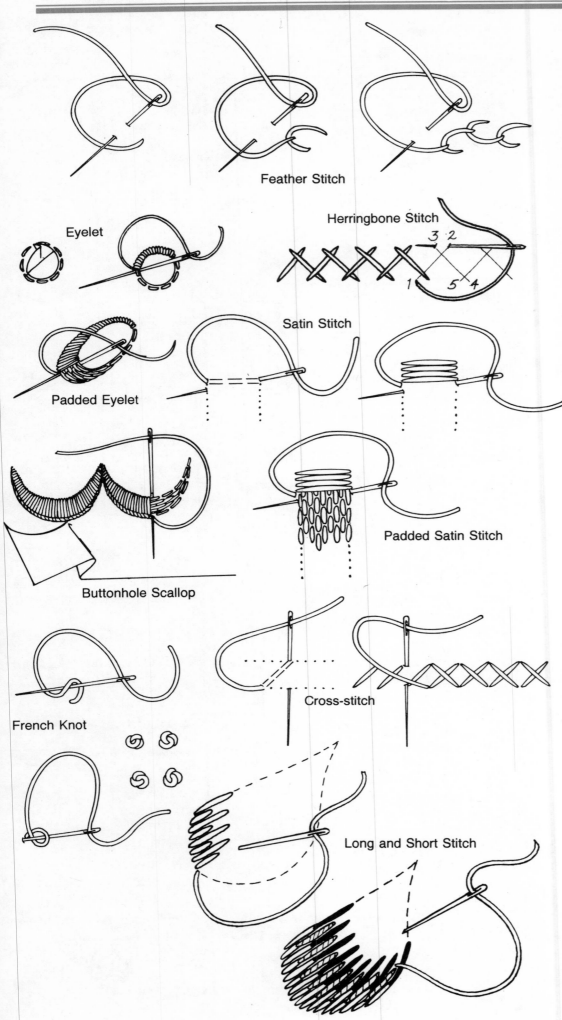

Feather Stitch

Eyelet

Herringbone Stitch

Padded Eyelet

Satin Stitch

Buttonhole Scallop

Padded Satin Stitch

French Knot

Cross-stitch

Long and Short Stitch

Embroidery on Knits

For hand embroidery on most knit fabrics, choose a fairly simple design as a heavily embroidered design will reduce the stretch in the garment and could also cause puckering or sagging in the design area. Observe the following procedure.

1. Transfer design to soft, lightweight backing fabric such as batiste.
2. Position design inside garment and baste in place.
3. Baste through backing and garment fabric along all design lines.
4. Work design keeping tension fairly loose.
5. Trim away excess backing close to stitches.
6. Press lightly.

Embroidery on bulky hand or machine knit fabrics may be done in the cross-stitch (page 108) or the duplicate stitch, illustrated below. For best coverage, select a yarn comparable in weight to the knit fabric. Work from a graph. Use one duplicate or cross-stitch to cover each knit stitch in the fabric.

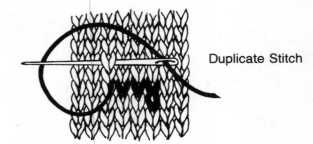

Duplicate Stitch

Embroidery With Mirrors (Shi-Sha or Shiska)

"Shi-sha" embroidery originated in Western India. The work is distinguished by the use of small mirrors which are held in place on the fabric with embroidery stitches. Mylar mirrors or pailettes with small holes (also called spangles) may be substituted for the traditional mica mirrors. These are available in craft shops. Use the mirrors for circular elements in a design such as flower centers and dots. Embroidery stitches traditionally used in this work include herringbone, chain, French knots, and the blanket stitch which is the basis of the method outlined below.

1. Transfer design to fabric. Indicate placement of mirrors with a dot.
2. Glue each mirror to fabric with a tiny dab of white glue. Pailettes may be sewn on with two or three small stitches.
3. Work a row of blanket stitches around the mirror with the loops next to the edge of the mirror.
4. Work another row of blanket stitches into the loops of the first row, again with the looped edge toward the center. Pull the thread fairly tight.
5. Repeat as many times as desired or necessary to

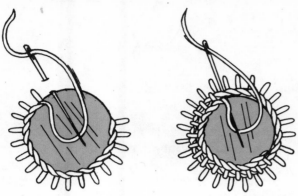

Stitching Around Mirror   Second Row Of Stitching

hold mirror securely in place. Use different colors
for the various rows of stitching for an interesting
effect.

6. To finish, run threads to edge of mirror and under
fabric to knot.

Embroidered Appliqués

Sometimes it may be advantageous to work embroidery
as an appliqué which can be removed for cleaning or used
on other garments. Historically, this embroidery was done
on net but you can use organdy, organza, or voile for the
same effect. It can also be done on ribbon.

1. Work on organza, organdy, voile, net, or ribbon
   stretched in an embroidery hoop.
2. When work is completed, clean and block.
3. Trim away excess backing to within ½″ of work (do
   not trim if on ribbon). Turn backing to wrong side
   of work. Clip curves, miter corners. Finger press
   backing hem in place and catchstitch all around.
4. Slipstitch embroidery to garment as desired.

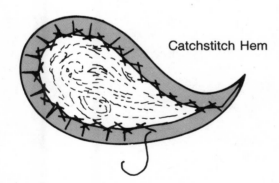

Catchstitch Hem

Cross-stitch Embroidery

Cross-stitch is a counted thread embroidery which traditionally required the use of an even-weave fabric as the
background cloth. Today, checked gingham is often the
fabric chosen for this work because the checks provide a
ready guide for the stitches which are usually placed in the

white squares. Interesting variations can be achieved by
locating some or all of the stitches in the colored squares.
Cross-stitch on gingham is a particularly easy technique for
beginning needleworkers. If you wish to work on a plain
colored fabric but prefer not to count threads for each
stitch, use the technique for cross-stitch on canvas discussed below. First read the following tips for cross-stitch.

☆ Cross-stitch is usually worked from a graph. Each
   graph square represents a counted square of fabric
   or, in the case of gingham, a check.

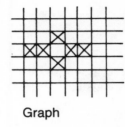 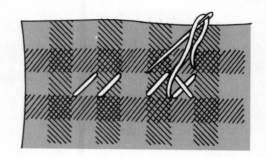

Graph

☆ Each symbol in a graph square represents a stitch.
   The symbols in the squares are often keyed to color
   schemes. See page 122 for the color symbols used
   on the design plates.
☆ Cross-stitch should be worked in horizontal rows.
   Work all the threads of the first half of the crosses
   in the same direction and make all the cross threads
   run in the opposite direction.

Cross-stitch on Canvas

This historic technique was used extensively during the
1920's when cross-stitch was a favorite form of needlework.
It is being done today with purchased kits, but you can
achieve the same results with any graphed design in this
book through the use of a soft, lightly sized mono canvas
for needlepoint. See page 121 for detailed information on
needlepoint canvas. The technique as outlined below eliminates thread counting and assures uniformity of stitches.
Although it was traditionally used only for cross-stitch,
other fancy needlepoint stitches like those illustrated on
page 121 could also be used.

1. Use inexpensive mono canvas, #8 or #10.
2. Prepare canvas as for needlepoint (see instructions
   for needlepoint). Transfer design to canvas using
   waterproof markers or work design from a graph.
3. Baste prepared canvas to right side of fabric align-
   ing grain of canvas with fabric grain.
4. Work in cross-stitch (or other needlepoint stitch).
   Stitch over canvas mesh through the fabric. Stitches
   should be taken in two motions: pull the needle and
   yarn through the fabric completely to the back of the

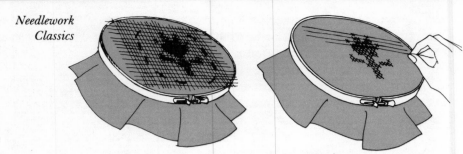

Canvas Basted In Place   Removing Canvas Threads

work, then complete the stitch by bringing the needle up to the right side. This is often referred to as the "stab" method of stitching and results in smoother, even-tensioned work. Do not pull stitches too tightly.

5. When work is completed, remove binding on edge of canvas and pull out canvas threads one by one. A tweezers may be helpful. If this step proves difficult, dampen work with sponge to soften the sizing in the canvas.

6. Block or lightly press completed work as required and complete project.

Punch-work

Punch-work is a type of counted thread embroidery in which holes are made in the fabric with a large needle. A lovely lacy effect is achieved by then pulling or distorting the weave and holding each hole in place with a series of perpendicular and diagonal stitches. The punched area is usually surrounded by embroidery of satin or stem stitching. To preserve the laciness of punch-work, avoid putting a facing behind the worked area. Substitute a self-bias binding or plan design placement to avoid faced areas.

Materials

Fabrics
Any loosely woven fabric in which the threads can be distorted and pulled without breaking is suitable. Examples are gauze, voile, some organdies and batistes.

Thread
Use strong cotton, linen, or polyester sewing thread for the punch-work and embroidery floss or other compatible thread or yarn for the embroidery.

Needles
Use a large, three-sided needle called a "glover's" or "sail maker's" needle. This needle is found in the notions department in home repair or utility needle assortments or in leather craft shops. A very large tapestry needle may also be used. For surrounding embroidery use suitable embroidery needle.

Hoop
An embroidery hoop is essential for holding fabric taut to preserve holes while they are being worked.

Basic Procedure for Punch-work

1. Prepare and press fabric. Transfer design to fabric. To space punch-work stitches, count threads as you work or mark a grid of dots spaced ¼" apart within the area to be punch-worked. Observe grainline carefully when marking dots. Assemble fabric in hoop.

2. Tie thread to eye of needle.

3. Complete punch-work following the illustrated steps below. On curved blocks, an extra stitch or two may be taken in a hole in order to include all dots. Do not omit any dots. If punch-work thread runs out in the middle of a row, make a knot in the threads on the wrong side of the work and run thread end under a few stitches before clipping. Tie new thread to existing stitches.

4. Complete surrounding embroidery.

5. When work is completed, clean, if necessary, and block or press.

6. Complete garment construction or resew ready-made garment.

Punch-work Stitch

1. Bring needle up from wrong side of fabric through first dot in second row. Leave long thread end. Go down through first dot in first row. Tie thread end to needle thread to secure. Pull thread tight.

2. Bring needle back up through first hole in second row. Pull thread tight.

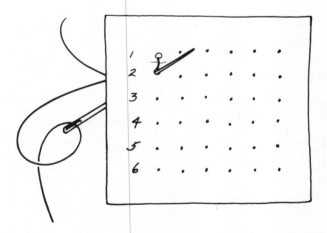

3. Insert needle into first hole in first row and diagonally back up through second dot in second row.

4. Insert needle into second dot in first row and back up through second hole in second row. Pull thread tight.

5. Insert needle into second hole in first row and diagonally up through third dot in second row. Continue to end of row.

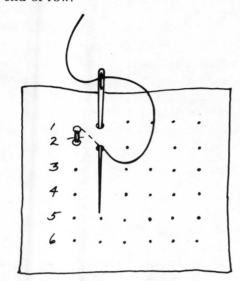

6. At end of row, bring needle up on second stitch through the last dot on the third row.

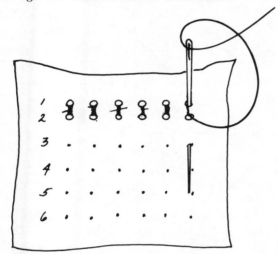

7. Working from right to left, proceed as before, carrying the needle diagonally from hole to dot after each stitch. Work is being done in rows 2 and 3. Continue from dot to dot, row to row.

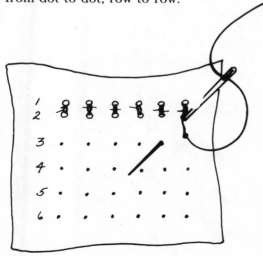

8. When entire block of dots is joined, turn work so that the same stitch can be done perpendicular to the first rows. For the purposes of working, the top becomes a side and a side becomes the top.

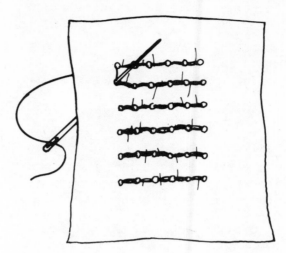

Braiding

Braiding is a type of embroidery in which cords, trims, ribbons, yarns, or similar materials are sewn to fabric by hand or machine to form designs. The design may be simple or complex, but the work is usually quite easy to do. Braid can be used to follow a linear design or to outline or fill in a motif. Linear designs should be braided before the garment is constructed so that ends can be enclosed in seams. In the case of ready-made garments, open seams to enclose braid ends, then resew. If braid cannot be worked into seams, plan endings and joinings to occur where they will not be noticed.

Braiding is usually applied directly to the garment but it may also be done as a removable appliqué. The directions for braided appliqués are essentially the same as for embroidered appliqués given on page 109.

Materials

Braid
For following designs, fairly narrow, flexible trims are most satisfactory. Try soutache, gimp, bias trims, narrow ribbons, wool and acrylic yarns, metallic yarns and threads, self-crocheted chains, and cording. To determine amount of braid needed, measure the design lines of one repeat, then multiply by the planned number of repeats. Add an extra yard.

Fabrics
Most fabrics are suitable background materials. The fabric must be firm enough to support the braided design. A single row of braid is appropriate for lightweight fabric whereas multiple rows might be too heavy and cause the fabric to droop.

Thread

Polyester or cotton sewing thread is suitable for attaching braid by hand or machine. Embroidery floss, yarns, and other suitable embroidery threads may be used for decorative couching.

Needles

Use sharps or embroidery needles compatible to the sewing thread or yarn being used. Use size 11 or 14 needles for machine stitching.

Basic Procedure for Braiding

1. Prepare and press fabric. Transfer design to fabric.
2. Arrange braid on fabric along design lines and pin or baste in place. Keep braid relaxed to prevent puckering. Ease braid around corners and curves. Miter flat braids at corners. To finish loose ends, thread fine cords or braids in a needle and pull through to wrong side of garment and tack in place. If braiding ends were not planned to end in a seam and the braid is too thick to pull through the fabric, plan endings and joinings to occur in an inconspicuous spot. Turn ends under and slipstitch in place.
3. Stitch braid in place checking position frequently. For narrow braid, stitch down center by hand or machine or couch by hand or machine zig-zag. For medium to wide braid, stitch along both edges.
4. When braiding is completed, clean item if necessary and block or press.
5. Construct garment or resew ready-made garment, if necessary.

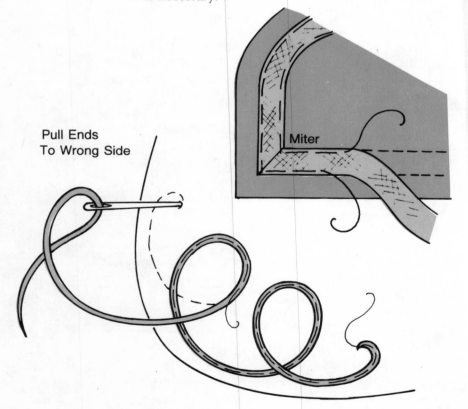

Pull Ends
To Wrong Side

Miter

Beading

Beading is the embroidery of elegance, involving as it does, an endless variety of beads, sequins, and pailettes in a fabulous array of glitter and color. Beads are sewn on individually with a few basic embroidery stitches or couched on in strings. Beading may also be worked as removable appliqués. The basic instructions are essentially the same as for embroidered appliqués discussed on page 109. When combining beading with other needlework techniques, sew beads on last.

Materials

Beads

Some of the many beads suitable for clothing are pearls, sequins and pailettes, seed, bugle, rocaille, faceted, lentil, and wooden beads. Rhinestones and nailheads which are set on with a tool are also used on clothing. Beads are available in a wide variety of colors and sizes and may be purchased loose in packages or tubes or in bunches of pre-strung strands. Buy enough beads to complete your project at the beginning. To figure number of beads needed, work a representative small portion of the design and count the number of beads used. Check care instructions. Many beads can be washed gently in mild soap. Some plastic items are heat-sensitive, some may be damaged in dry cleaning. Metal-lined beads may tarnish.

Fabrics

Most fabrics are suitable for beading. Consider the ability of the fabric to support the weight of the beads when planning the project. On soft flimsy fabrics, use a lightweight backing. With sheers use a double layer of fabric. The heaviness of the design will be determined by the size and weight of the beads and the density of the placement. Satin, linen, and peau-de-soie are suitable for massive interpretations; silk, organza, and crepe-de-chine call for lighter beading.

Thread

Use waxed silk or mercerized cotton thread or nylon thread. Color should be suited to background fabric and to beads.

Needles, Pins, Beeswax

Special beading needles are available in craft shops. They are long, thin, and pliable. Regular sewing needles may be used for couching. Use fine thin pins for arranging beads in the design. Use beeswax from the notions department to smooth and strengthen thread used for beading.

Beading Stitches

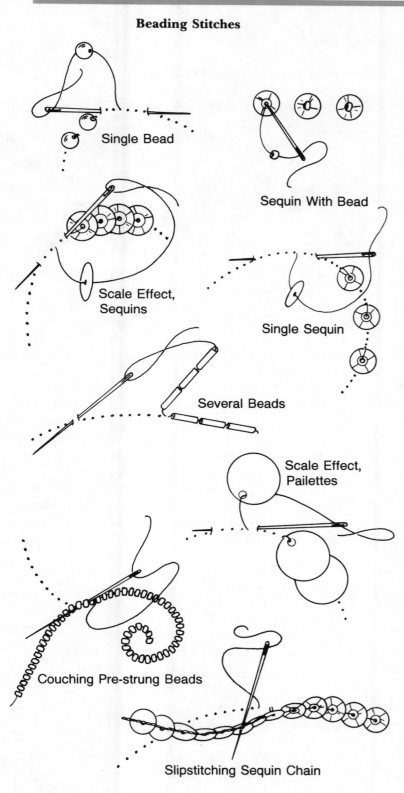

Single Bead

Sequin With Bead

Scale Effect, Sequins

Single Sequin

Several Beads

Scale Effect, Pailettes

Couching Pre-strung Beads

Slipstitching Sequin Chain

attaching single beads, a short double strand for attaching or stringing groups. Use even tension; beads should neither pucker fabric nor droop. On sheer fabrics, move thread from one design area to another through beads whenever possible. Settle each bead into place before securing to be sure position is exactly as desired.

4. When beading is completed, clean if necessary and block or press.
5. Construct garment or resew ready-made garment. Use a zipper foot to sew seams in beaded area.
6. Fill in any spaces at seams with additional beads, if necessary.

There are two ways to use beading on needlepoint canvas. One method is to embellish a worked needlepoint canvas with beads. After the canvas is blocked, apply a bead at every needlepoint stitch in the design area to be beaded. Use the half-cross stitch. For needlepoint beading directly on needlepoint canvas, see page 123.

Quilting

Quilting is an historic method of joining layers of fabric together. It was originally used to create a warm fabric and was most often constructed with a top fabric, a filler, and a backing fabric stitched together by hand following an ornamental pattern. It was a time-consuming technique which is more quickly accomplished with a sewing machine today. Quilting designs may be geometric, floral, or abstract in nature, but they often follow the outlines of patchwork or appliqué designs. Use quilting to provide additional warmth in jackets and coats, to add weight at hemlines, or to add subtle surface interest on an otherwise plain fabric.

Quilting may be done in an all over pattern on fabric before constructing a completely quilted garment, or it may be used for accent in areas such as cuffs, yokes, lapels, and necklines. Extensively quilted fabrics are bulky and may result in a closer-than-desired fit if the pattern is not selected carefully. Choose a pattern designed for quilted fabric, or select a style with a looser fit. When using an ordinary pattern, cut the garment slightly larger.

Since quilting causes fabric to draw up, it will be necessary to purchase more fabric than the planned project would normally require. Allow an extra 1/4 yard for each major garment piece to be quilted in an all over pattern.

Basic Procedure for Beading

1. Prepare and press fabric. Transfer design to fabric. Assemble fabric in hoop.
2. Fasten thread securely at beginning and end of stitching on wrong side of work.
3. Choose the appropriate stitch (see illustrations) to attach beads. Use a short single strand of thread for

Materials

Fabric
Almost any fabric can be quilted for clothing and accessories. Firmly woven, smooth and crisp fabrics such as flannel, broadcloth, poplin, denim, and satin are easiest to handle. Other fabrics including velvet and velveteen can be quilted with difficulty, but the truly ele-

gant results may be worth the effort. Other suitable fabrics include challis, knits, and wool crepe. Plan to do machine quilting on particularly heavy fabrics. For backing fabrics, select smooth, fairly lightweight fabrics. Underlining fabrics and organza work well as backing fabrics in articles of clothing.

Filler

Select polyester fiberfill or batting as it is washable. Lightweight flannel is also appropriate.

Thread

Use quilting thread, #50 cotton thread, buttonhole twist or polyester thread. Traditionally, white thread was used for quilting but contemporary quilters can create novel effects with threads of contrasting colors.

Needles

For hand quilting use size 8 or 10 sharps. On thick, heavy fabrics try a curved upholstery needle. For machine quilting on most fabrics, use size 14 or 16 machine needles.

Basic Procedure for Quilting Fabric Before Garment Construction

1. If you are planning a garment with all over quilting, cut large rectangles of fabric, backing, and filler which will accomodate each major pattern piece. Do not quilt facings. Rectangles should be cut at least 3″ larger all around than the widest part of the pattern piece. Be sure to cut rectangles on grain to insure proper pattern placement when quilting is completed.
2. Mark the quilting design directly onto the right side of each garment section to be quilted. Use pencil, chalk, or dressmaker's carbon.
3. Assemble pieces. Place backing right side down on a smooth surface. Spread batting or fiberfill over backing. Place top fabric right side up over filler. Be sure there are no wrinkles in any layer.

4. Pin baste the layers together using many pins. Pin basting is adequate for hand quilting. For machine quilting, thread basting is advisable. Baste from the center out or in a grid, as illustrated.

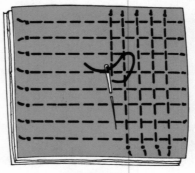 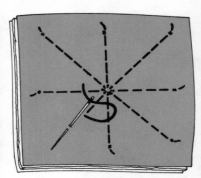

Grid Basting   Radial Basting

5. *To quilt by hand,* use a quilting hoop to hold work taut. Move the hoop from section to section until the work is complete. For small pieces of work use an ordinary embroidery hoop. Begin quilting by tying a small knot in the end of the thread and passing the needle through all three layers from backing to top. Tug gently so the knot passes through the backing into the batting. Take small, even running stitches along the marked quilting lines. Stitch with one hand above and one hand below the quilt to be sure the needle goes through all layers. To end stitching, tie a knot in the thread close to the fabric surface. Take one more stitch and pull knot into batting. Pass thread off into batting. Bring the needle out and clip thread closely.

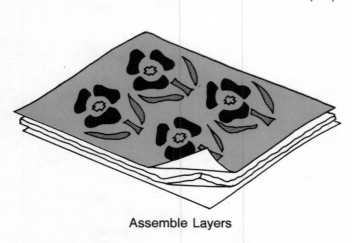

Assemble Layers

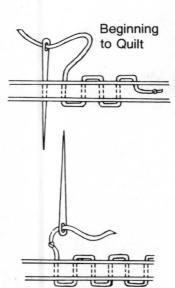

Beginning
to Quilt

Ending Stitching

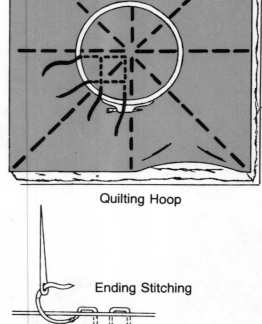

Quilting Hoop

6. *For machine quilting,* adjust tension and pressure on machine to accomodate the layered fabrics. Experiment on a layered test swatch. Machine stitch along quilting pattern lines using a straight, zig-zag, or other decorative stitch. Use the quilting foot for your machine as it rides easily over layers. For very large pieces, roll excess fabric to make handling at the machine less cumbersome. On large projects, stitch from the center of the piece toward the edges smoothing fabric toward the edges and away from the foot as you stitch. Do not backstitch. Pull threads to wrong side of work and tie securely.

7. When quilting is completed, press work lightly. Cut garment sections from quilted fabric in single layers and assemble garment or accessory. To reduce bulk in seams, darts, and zipper plackets on heavily quilted items, gently remove the filler from these areas after stitching. Hems edges may be handled in the same manner or bound with self or contrasting bias binding.

Quilting On Completed Garments

Adding a quilted motif to a completed garment is an easy way to enhance otherwise plain clothing. Choose simple motifs to quilt around the neckline of a dress, on the front of a cotton T-shirt, or at the hemline of a skirt. The possibilities are numerous.

1. Transfer design to right side of garment in desired position.
2. Cut a layer of fiberfill and a piece of soft underlining fabric 1″ larger than the design all around. Position filler and backing under design on wrong side of garment and baste in place.
3. Quilt by hand or machine as outlined in steps 5 and 6, above.
4. When quilting is completed, trim away excess filler close to stitching and pink edges of backing.

Trapunto

Trapunto is a form of quilting in which a design or part of a design is padded with cording or fiberfill inserted through slits in the backing fabric. The design may be stitched by hand or machine and the padding adds dimension to the finished work. Trapunto may be executed during garment construction or worked on a ready-made garment.

Materials

Fabric
This work is best done on smooth, closely woven fabrics. Knits are also particularly suited to this technique as their inherent "give" eliminates puckering. For the

backing, use a firmly woven fabric in a lighter weight. Lining and underlining fabrics are suitable.

Stuffing
Use cotton, acrylic, or polyester cords and yarns to cord narrow areas and polyester fiberfill or batting for larger areas. The use of brightly colored stuffing materials creates interesting effects on sheer fabrics.

Thread
Use polyester or cotton sewing threads. For added interest, try buttonhole twist. Embroidery floss may be used for a decorative touch if work is done by hand.

Needles
For hand sewing, choose sharps in size 8 or 10. For corded quilting, use a tapestry or rug needle. Use size 14 needles for machine stitchery.

Basic Procedure for Trapunto During Garment Construction

1. Prepare and press fabrics. Since trapunto may draw up fabric in length and width, cut pieces substantially larger than the pattern piece. Allow at least 2″ extra all around.
2. Transfer design to fabric or trace design onto tissue paper and baste to fabric in planned position. Layer and baste fabric and backing together.
3. Stitch along design lines by machine or by hand with closely spaced running stitches. Other decorative stitches may also be used. Do not backstitch; instead, draw thread ends to wrong side and knot. Do not allow stitching lines to cross. Move the machine wheel by hand around complicated or extremely curved design lines.

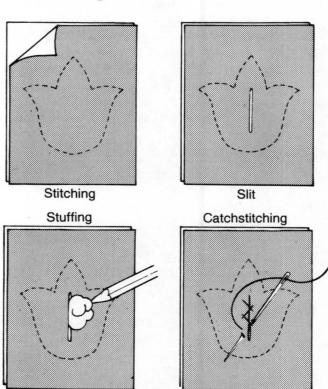

Stitching   Slit

Stuffing   Catchstitching

4. Remove basting and stuff or cord the design areas. *To stuff,* slit the backing fabric in several places and poke stuffing material into design with a knitting needle, tweezers, or the eye end of a large tapestry needle. To avoid puckers, do not overstuff. Close the slit with catchstitching. *To cord* areas outlined with parallel lines of stitching, insert needle through backing only, between lines of stitching. To ease cord smoothly around curves, angles, or points, bring needle out and reinsert it at the same place leaving a little cording outside the backing. When completed, trim all cord ends to about ⅛".

5. Lightly press work, pin pattern pieces in place, cut, and construct item following pattern instructions.

6. Finished trapunto should be lined for a neat appearance and to protect it in washing and wearing.

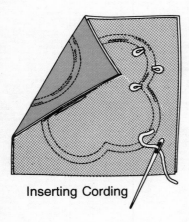

Inserting Cording

Trapunto on Ready-made Clothing

1. Since elaborate designs worked in trapunto may affect the garment size, it is essential to choose a simple motif with a minimum of corded areas.

2. Follow the basic procedure for trapunto as outlined in steps 1 through 4, above. Cut backing fabric 2" larger than the design all around. If garment is underlined, utilize the underlining as the backing.

3. Stuff design area lightly.

4. To protect slits made for stuffing purposes from raveling, a small piece of woven, fusible (iron-on) interfacing may be placed over the slits and fused in place.

Appliqué

Appliqué is a form of textile embroidery in which designs are created by attaching one fabric to another. Appliqué may be done by machine for durability or by hand with invisible or visible stitches. Simple basic appliqué is a quick and easy way to add a bold area of color to a garment. The use of complex shapes and exotic methods such as reverse and shadow appliqué creates unusual effects.

For this form of needlework, choose bold, uncomplicated designs rather than tiny, detailed ones. Remember that detail and linear qualities can be added to bold shapes with embroidery, braiding, beading, or quilting. Appliqué shapes can also be lightly stuffed with fiberfill before stitching is completed to add surface interest.

Materials

Fabric

Many fabrics are suitable for appliqué, among them percale, broadcloth, lightweight linen, wool, felt, and leather. Sheer fabrics like organdy and voile can be used to create soft, subtle effects. The fabric should be equal in weight to or lighter than the background fabric to which it will be sewn.

Yarn

For hand appliqué and machine appliqué, use either polyester or mercerized cotton sewing thread. When embroidery stitches are combined with appliqué, any thread or yarn suitable for embroidery can be used. Using a fusible bonding agent (see below) eliminates thread except for embroidery stitches that may be added to enhance the appliqué.

Needles

Use sharps for hand appliqué. Use embroidery/crewel needles for embroidery. Use size 14 needles for machine appliqué.

Fusibles

A fusible bonding agent is a lightweight, thermoplastic web that joins two fabrics by fusing when heat, moisture, and pressure are applied with an iron. These bonding agents are marketed in several widths and lengths and are usually available where fabrics are sold. (Current brand names of this material include Pellon Fusible Web, Stacy Stitch Witchery, Poly Bond by Coats and Clark, and Armo Stylus Fusible Web.)

Basic Procedure for Appliqué with Turned Edge

1. Transfer design to background fabric for placement of each shape to be appliquéd. Transfer individual shapes to selected fabrics and add ¼" turn-under allowance to each appliqué.

2. Stitch around each appliqué by hand or machine ¼" from the edge.

3. Turn edges of appliqué to wrong side on stitched line and press lightly. Clip curves and miter corners and points as illustrated to create a smooth edge.

4. Pin appliqués in position on background fabric and stitch in place by hand or machine. Use a straight or zig-zag stitch close to the edge for machine appliqué. For hand stitching, use the slipstitch, run-

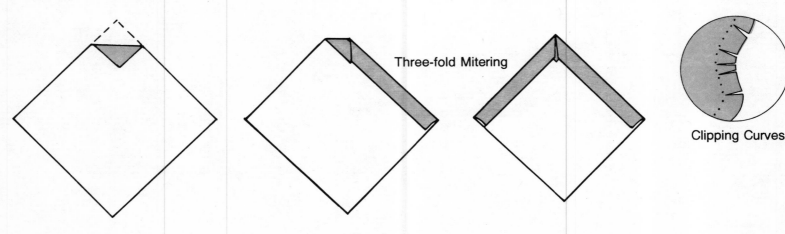

Three-fold Mitering

Clipping Curves

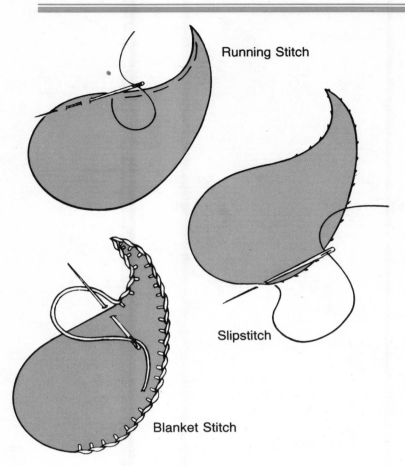

Running Stitch

Slipstitch

Blanket Stitch

ning stitch, or a decorative stitch like blanket or chain stitch. If desired, add embroidered details.

Basic Procedure for Appliqué with Raw Edge

1. Transfer design to background fabric for placement guide. Transfer individual shapes to selected fabrics and cut out appliqués.
2. Position individual appliqués on background fabric and baste in place by hand or machine with straight or zig-zag stitch.
3. Sew design in place using a machine satin stitch (tightly spaced zig-zag stitch) enclosing all raw edges with stitches. For hand work, substitute tightly spaced blanket stitches. Add embroidered details if desired.

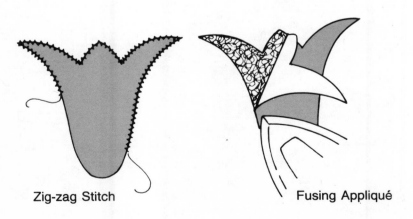

Zig-zag Stitch

Fusing Appliqué

Basic Procedure for Appliqué with Fusibles

1. Transfer design to background fabric, appliqué fabric, and fusible web. Do not add turn-under allowances. Carefully cut shapes from appliqué fabric and fusible web.
2. Place fusible web between the appliqué and background fabric and follow product directions for fusing. (A paper towel placed between the iron and the appliqué will help prevent the bonding agent from sticking to the iron soleplate.) Allow work to cool on the ironing board to prevent unbonding, wrinkling, or shifting that could occur until the agent is completely cool.
3. Add embroidery stitches by hand or machine to further enhance the appliqué. However, fusibles tend to stiffen fabric making hand embroidery more difficult to execute.

Reverse Appliqué

This needlework technique originated with a Panamanian Indian Tribe. The work was used for yokes on the women's traditional "mola" or blouse. Reverse appliqué may be sewn into a garment during construction like any other fabric or it may be sewn on as an appliqué or band. Use this technique to create beautiful pockets for skirts, pants, and tote bags, for example.

The traditional method for this form of appliqué is to cut away and narrowly hem shapes within shapes. A design for reverse appliqué must be segmented or contain shapes within shapes. Usually, the shapes should be at least ¼″ apart. When lightweight fabrics like percale or broadcloth are being used, three to five layers of fabric can be worked. With heavier fabrics like felt or fake suede, use fewer layers because it might be difficult to stitch through too many layers. Plan color distribution on a tracing of the design or with colored paper.

1. Arrange fabric in layers as desired. The bottom layer will remain uncut and serve as the backing fabric. The top layer will probably be the predominant color.
2. Transfer design shapes to be cut out of top layer onto fabric. Transfer shapes within shapes as you work.
3. Baste the layers together around the edges and diagonally across the center in both directions.

Segmented Design

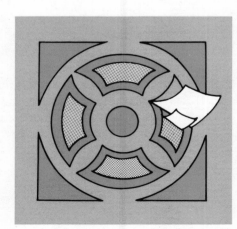

Removing Layers

Shape-Within-Shape

4. With sharp pointed embroidery scissors, pierce top layer of fabric and cut away shapes. If you are working a large or complicated design, cut one shape at a time. For a turned edge, allow ¼″ all around design line for turn-under. Clip corners and curves. Slit areas too small to be cut out. For an unturned edge, cut on exact design lines.

5. Stitch edges in place through all layers. For turned edges, turn edge under with tip of needle as you sew. Use slipstitch or an embroidery stitch. For un-

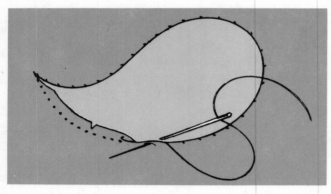

Slipstitching A Turned Edge

turned edges, stitch close to edge by hand or machine. Machine satin stitch may also be used.

6. Cut out shapes to expose progressive layers and proceed as above. Fold hems of top layers over edges of underlying ones when cutting away several layers at one time.

Shadow Appliqué

Shadow appliqué is used to apply sheer designs to sheer fabrics such as voile, organza, lightweight silks, organdy, and batiste. The technique is beautifully suited for scarves, blouses, lingerie, stoles, skirts, or any other item which might be interpreted in sheer fabric. Appliqués can be done in the same color as the background fabric or in one or more different colors. Thread should match the fabric chosen for appliqué.

1. Transfer design to background fabric and appliqué fabric. Match grainlines. When working appliqué in one color, transfer complete design to one large piece of appliqué fabric and treat as a single unit. If appliqué is to be done in more than one color, transfer individual design elements to appropriate fabrics and cut each with a generous margin of fabric all around.

2. Position appliqué on background fabric. Carefully hand baste in place.

3. Machine stitch each design element in place just inside the design lines.

4. Satin stitch by machine along design lines, covering first row of machine stitching.

5. Carefully trim away excess fabric from around appliqués close to stitching.

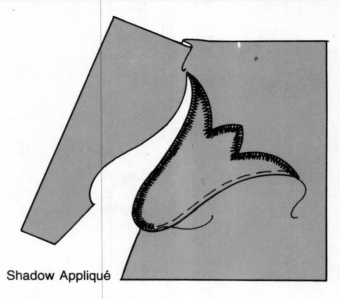

Shadow Appliqué

Floating Appliqué (Three-Dimensional)

To create an appliqué which moves, try this method. It is perfect for leaves, butterflies, and flowers. Children will love it. Any lightweight, firmly woven fabric is suitable and sheers are especially lovely handled in this manner. Simple solid shapes work best.

1. Transfer design to appliqué fabric. On garment, mark only the center point of each appliqué.

2. With wrong sides together, pin individual appliqués to a second layer of self fabric or a layer of matching lightweight lining fabric, matching grains. Cut out design area, allowing a generous margin all around.

3. Machine stitch along design lines.

4. Machine satin stitch over first row of stitching.

5. Trim away excess fabric around design taking care not to cut into satin stitch. Cut as close to satin stitch as possible.

Floating Appliqué

6. Pin appliqué to garment at positioning point. Stitch appliqué to garment at positioning point by hand. Decorative stitches such as French knots may be used.

Patchwork

Patchwork is a very old method for forming a large piece of fabric from many smaller ones. It can be done in two ways. Appliquéd patchwork is done by applying fabric shapes in a pattern to a background fabric. When shapes of fabric are sewn to each other to form a new, larger shape, the work is called piecework. Piecework is often done in blocks which are then set together to form a cloth. Traditionally, patchwork was used to create quilts, but it is an interesting form of needlework to incorporate in clothing and accessories. These may be cut entirely or in part from patchwork cloth. They may also be decorated with a single design element from a patchwork design, with a complete block, or with a group of blocks. Appliquéd patchwork may be done on a backing piece cut in the desired garment shape.

A garment composed entirely of patchwork fabric should be carefully planned. Choose simple styles with few seams and darts as the fabric should be the primary point of interest. Remember that patchwork may be heavy if composed of many very small pieces or bulky if made of thick fabrics. Position garment pattern pieces on patchwork fabric so that horizontal lines will match at sides and centers. Cut facings, waistbands, and similar inside pieces of plain fabric to reduce bulk. Line patchwork clothing to protect the seams from raveling and for added wearing comfort.

The instructions which follow are for pieced patchwork. For appliquéd patchwork designs, see basic procedure for appliqué.

Materials

Fabrics
The traditional fabric for patchwork was cotton, but, with careful planning, other fabrics may also be used. Try cotton or cotton blends in dress or shirt weight fabric. Other possibilities include silks, corduroy, velveteen, and lightweight wools. Fabric types may be mixed if they are of similar weights. Underline very lightweight fabrics for added weight. If an entire patchwork garment is planned, avoid bulky or loosely woven fabrics. Use light to medium weight fabrics for backing. Lining and underlining fabrics are also appropriate for backings.

Thread
For both machine and hand piecing, use cotton or polyester thread in a neutral or matching shade.

Needles
Use size 8 to 10 sharps for hand piecing. Use size 14 machine needle for machine piecing.

Basic Procedure for Pieced Patchwork

1. Preshrink and press all fabrics whether newly purchased or recycled scraps. Transfer design parts to appropriate fabrics using the template method on page 14. Be sure to add seam allowances of ¼" all around each piece. Observe grainlines.
2. Cut pieces carefully. Piecework requires precise measuring and cutting of design elements.
3. Begin by joining one small unit to another. Then join that unit to another and continue until large sections of completed patchwork can be joined. Press each seam open or to one side before crossing it with another.

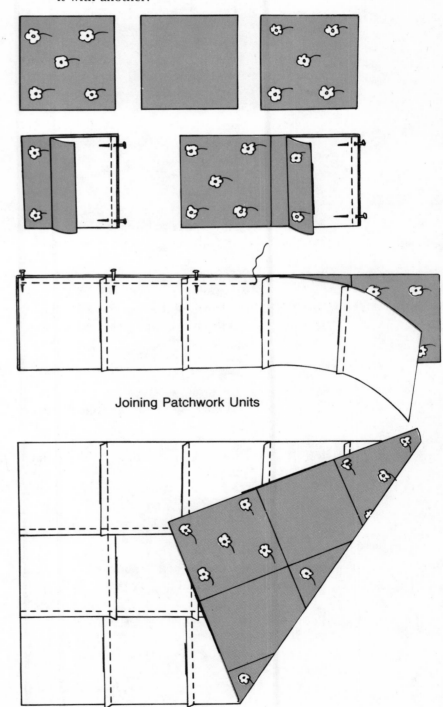

Joining Patchwork Units

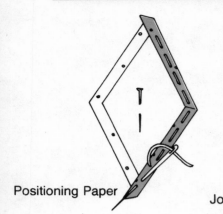

Positioning Paper

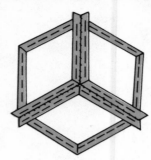

Joining With Whipstitching

Joining Completed

Masking Tape
Stitching Guide

To piece by hand, use a small running stitch. Begin with a knot or small backstitch and continue taking three or four stitches. End with a backstitch. For hexagons, parallelograms, and other pieces that have bias edges, paper patterns are helpful in piecing and maintaining the shape. Cut a number of paper patterns exactly the size and shape of the finished patchwork piece. Use construction paper or paper of a similar weight. Center paper pattern on cut fabric and fold seam allowances over paper. Baste through seam allowances, paper, and fabric. Join by holding two pieces with right sides together. Whipstitch along the edge to be joined. Take special care matching and stitching corners. To remove paper patterns, clip basting. The paper patterns can be used several times.

To piece by machine, join units and stitch using 10 to 12 stitches per inch. Guide pieces carefully with cut edge against the appropriate seam allowance on the throat plate. Masking tape can be applied to the throat plate for a stitching guide as shown. Since each seam will be crossed by another seam, backstitching is not necessary.

4. Press completed work and use in garment construction as planned.

Using Patchwork Fabric in Garment Construction

To minimize waste and time spent in constructing garments or portions of garments from patchwork cloth, construct patchwork in sizes just large enough to contain garment units.

Patchwork Garments and Garment Sections
1. Press pattern pieces and lay out to estimate patchwork yardage needed.
2. Piece together the required yardage in a shape roughly like garment piece or in a rectangle that will accomodate the pattern piece. Press completed work.
3. Position pattern pieces on completed patchwork fabric. Align grainlines and cut.

4. Construct item treating patchwork like any other fabric. Underline each piece or line garment with a separate lining.

Completed patchwork blocks, groups of blocks, bands, and strips may be applied (appliquéd) to home-sewn and ready-made garments as appliqués.

Placement of vertical bands of completed patchwork should follow grainline whenever possible. They should be applied during garment construction in order to enclose the ends at the neckline, waistline, and/or hemline. They can be applied to completed garments following the procedure for applied patchwork outlined below.

Horizontal bands of patchwork are more difficult to use in garment construction because the taper of the side seams interferes with the smooth continuity of the patchwork design. This is especially true with very bias garment sections. The beauty of patchwork lies in its strict geometry and care should be taken in placement to avoid disrupting the design. Therefore, horizontal bands of patchwork are best suited for use as cuffs, waistbands, and straps and to enhance the edges of straight or nearly straight slacks, sleeves, and gathered skirts.

Applied Patchwork
1. Complete patchwork in desired shape following basic procedure for pieced patchwork.
2. Press under ¼" all around outside edges of work.
3. Position on garment and baste or pin in place.
4. Sew in place with slipstitching or machine stitching close to folded edge.
5. If the addition of a patchwork band or blocks adds excess bulk, cut away garment fabric behind applied patchwork to within ½" of stitching lines.

It is possible to cover small areas of ready-made clothing with patchwork fabric. Yokes, collars, cuffs, and bands are most appropriate. To make a pattern of the area, pin tracing paper to the section and carefully outline the shape. Add ¼" all around for a turn-under allowance. Use tracing as a pattern for patchwork and apply patchwork to garment as outlined above.

Needlepoint

Needlepoint is counted thread embroidery done on even-weave fabric or stiff canvas. Various types of needlepoint are related to the size of the canvas mesh (petit point, gros point) and the resulting number of stitches necessary to cover it. Needlepoint on canvas creates a sturdy, fairly stiff, long-wearing cloth, suitable for many uses. Needlepoint designs can be enhanced with the addition of beads or embroidery stitches.

Materials

Canvas

Needlepoint canvas is a cotton fabric woven in open, regular squares and stiffened for body and easy stitching. The size of canvas describes the number of mesh (threads) per inch. For example, #10 canvas has 10 mesh to the inch while #16 canvas has 16 mesh to the inch. Canvas ranges in size from very coarse, #3, to very fine, #40 and is sold by the yard.

Duo (Penelope) canvas has two threads for each mesh so that it can be split for finer detail or be used for petit point.

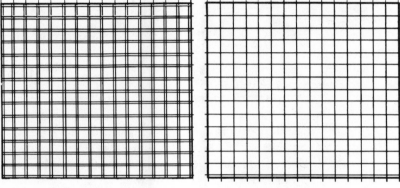

Duo (Penelope) Canvas   Mono Canvas

Mono canvas has one thread for each mesh and is suitable for many designs. Bargello should always be worked on mono canvas.

Yarn

Many yarns in a wide array of colors are available for needlepoint. Most salesclerks can help you estimate the amount of yarn needed, so take the design with you to purchase yarn. Needlepoint yarn calculators are also available. Or, you can estimate the amount needed yourself. Simply calculate the number of square inches to be covered by each color. Make generous estimates for oddly shaped areas. Multiply the number of square inches for each color by the amount of yarn needed to cover one square inch of canvas. Since this amount will vary with the stitch used and the canvas size (mesh per inch), it will be necessary to work a square inch of canvas to determine how much yarn it takes. Always buy enough yarn to finish a project since it may be difficult to match color later on.

The yarns most commonly used for needlepoint are Persian wool, tapestry wool, and crewel yarn. Persian wool is a three-stranded yarn which can be divided for use on several canvas sizes. Tapestry wool is a tightly twisted, four-ply yarn which is not easily separated and is not used on canvas smaller than 14 mesh per inch. Crewel yarn, a fine, two-ply yarn, can be used with several threads together to cover many different canvas sizes. Other yarn possibilities include rug wool, embroidery floss, metallic yarns, pearl cotton, chenille, and silk floss.

Needles

Use tapestry needles.

Stitches

The three stitches most often used for needlepoint are the continental, basket weave, and half cross. All three create the same appearance on the surface of the work. The half cross-stitch requires the least amount of yarn and results in the thinnest completed fabric which makes it a good choice for belts and other items of clothing. It is also used for needlepoint pictures and articles which will receive little wear. It should be worked only on duo (Penelope) canvas. The continental stitch and the basket weave stitch require more yarn because they create a padded effect on the back of the work which increases the durability and wearing qualities of the finished work. Use either of these stitches on handbags where long-wearing is an important quality. Continental stitch is best used for outlining, for working fine details, and for filling in small areas. If it is used for the entire work, the canvas will become badly misshapen and require extensive blocking. The basket weave stitch is recommended for filling in backgrounds as well as any other areas of the design. For clothing, stitches with short floats are most suitable as they resist pulling and snagging.

The Stitches

The needlepoint stitches illustrated here are some of the basic and most often used. There are many others. The stitch illustrations are numbered for easy translation.

Odd numbers indicate that the needle is coming to the front of the work at the beginning of a stitch.

Even numbers indicate that the needle is going to the back of the canvas at the completion of a stitch.

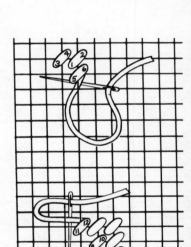

Basket Weave Stitch

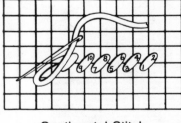

Continental Stitch

Cross-stitch

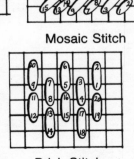

Mosaic Stitch

Byzantine Stitch

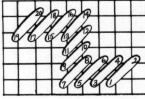

Half Cross-stitch

Brick Stitch

The color used on the graphs which appear on several design plates are suggestions only. Samples which appear in color photography were not necessarily worked in the same colors as those which appear on the graphs since individual color preference dictates color choice.

Graph Color Key

WHITE

LIGHT GREY

DARK GREY

BLACK

FLESH

BEIGE

BROWN

LIGHT YELLOW

MEDIUM YELLOW

DARK YELLOW

ORANGE

LIGHT PINK

PINK

DARK PINK

LIGHT RED

MEDIUM RED

DARK RED

MAUVE

PURPLE

LIGHT GREEN

MEDIUM GREEN

DARK GREEN

LIGHT BLUE

MEDIUM BLUE

DARK BLUE

TURQUOISE

Basic Procedure for Needlepoint

1. Cut canvas to size allowing at least a two-inch border all around for blocking, mounting, and stitch shrinkage (canvas is drawn up when stitches are taken). Bind the edges with masking tape to prevent raveling and to make the canvas easier to hold.

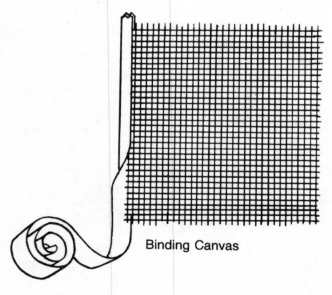

Binding Canvas

2. Transfer design to canvas or work from a graph. To read a graph remember that each square represents an intersection of threads in the canvas. Always count intersections of the canvas threads (mesh) not holes in the canvas. When working from a graph, locate the center of the graph and the center of the canvas and begin there.

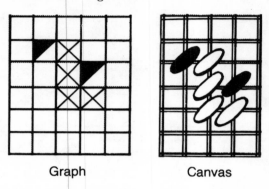

Graph   Canvas

3. Before you begin to stitch, try the yarn, stitches, and needle to be certain that all function well together to cover the canvas smoothly and easily. To begin stitching, tie a knot in the end of a piece of yarn and pass the yarn from the right side to the underside of the canvas about one-half inch from the beginning point within the design area. Take a few stitches along the row catching the yarn with each

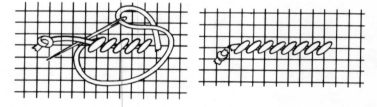

Starting A Piece Of Yarn

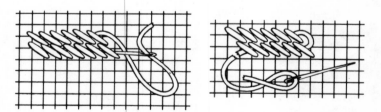

Ending A Piece Of Yarn

stitch. When you reach the knot, clip it off. The yarn will be secured on the underside by the stitches. As you finish each yarn, pass the yarn end under a few stitches on the back of the work. Begin and end subsequent yarns by passing the yarn end under a few stitches on the back of the work. Begin working in the center of the canvas and work the design areas first and the background last. Add beads or embroidery after canvas is blocked. If the design includes curves and diagonals, remember that needlepoint canvas is basically geometric and that curves and diagonals are made up of small geometric steps that give the appearance of a curve.

Interaction Of Curves And Diagonals On Graph

4. When needlepoint is completed, clean if necessary and block or press into shape.

Needlepoint Beading

Especially beautiful and novel effects are easily achieved by incorporating beads with needlepoint stitches. This technique is particularly appropriate for small accessory items like evening bags, belts, and hat bands, but could also be used in small areas on garments for pockets, collars, cuffs, or yokes.

1. Prepare duo (Penelope) canvas following the basic procedure for needlepoint.
2. First work the needlepoint areas where beads will not be located using the half cross-stitch.
3. To work beaded areas, use a fine beading needle and a double knotted thread in a color to match the

beads used. Whenever the size of the bead hole permits, use yarn or embroidery floss in place of thread. Bring needle up through canvas as for regular needlepoint, string on one bead and work in continental stitch.

4. Complete design incorporating a bead with each stitch. To keep work smooth and flat, keep tension even. If canvas tends to buckle, it may be necessary to work a stitch without a bead occasionally.
5. Block finished work and complete construction of item.

Needlepoint Cloth for Garment Sections

It is possible to substitute needlepoint for fabric in a garment area such as yoke, cuffs or belt. Remember that needlepoint will be stiff and won't give or ease so small sections are the best place to try this. Jackets, hats, shoes, handbags, and other accessories constructed with needlepoint canvas substituted for fabric in selected areas are available in many needlework stores. You could construct a similar item and then work the needlepoint but a better idea is to work the needlepoint piece first, then block the finished piece and treat it like any other fabric in attaching it to a garment.

1. Prepare canvas. Place pattern piece under canvas. Align grainline marking with a lengthwise thread in canvas. Pin pattern in place and draw onto canvas using waterproof pen. Trace cutting lines, darts, and buttonholes. Allow at least two inches extra all around piece, cut and bind canvas.
2. Transfer design to canvas. Position design under canvas matching lengthwise direction of design with lengthwise thread in canvas. If necessary, flop design for symmetrical repeat and align the design on a horizontal canvas thread all the way across. Design should not extend into darts, buttonholes, or seam allowances.
3. Work design. Extend stitches into seam allowances

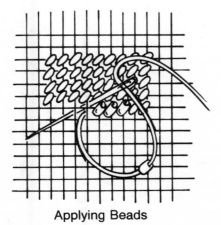

Applying Beads

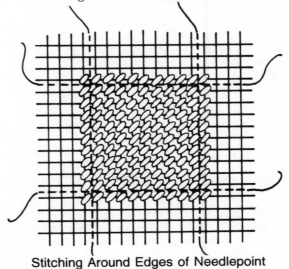

Stitching Around Edges of Needlepoint

and just over the marked lines into the dart. Do not work in buttonhole areas.

4. Block completed work based on pattern shape traced onto paper. Add stitches wherever shrinkage has made the worked piece smaller than pattern piece.

5. Machine stitch twice around the edges of the piece using a short stitch. Trim excess canvas to ½" all around.

6. Complete garment construction incorporating completed needlepoint. Stitch on the needlepoint side when completing seams and keep stitching just on the edge of the needlepoint stitches to prevent unworked canvas from showing at seams. Bind exposed rough seam edges in garment.

Needlepoint Cloth Variation

This technique creates a softer, fluffier needlepoint fabric by removing the sizing from the canvas after the piece is worked. Since yarn dyes are unpredictable (some run, some pull color from their neighbors) and since there is certain to be shrinkage with this method, it is *imperative* that you work and test wash a swatch first using the colors in their planned sequence.

1. Follow steps 1 through 5, above but work needlepoint an extra inch beyond the cutting line.

2. When work is completed, dip entire piece in warm water for a minute. Remove and dip a few more times.

3. Roll in a towel to blot, then block. Check shape against pattern piece. When dry, check against pattern piece for size and fill in any blank spots with extra stitches.

4. Proceed with garment construction as outlined in step 6, above.

Needlepoint Appliqué

Use this technique to create removable needlepoint pieces for a pocket, patch, or appliqué. The finishing methods described below may be used for belts, hat bands, collars, cuffs, or anything which should be backed.

Prepare canvas and work needlepoint following the basic procedure for needlepoint, above. After blocking, machine stitch around completed work and finish in the following manner.

1. Trim canvas to 1" all around. Clip curves.

2. Turn unworked canvas to wrong side of work, miter corners when necessary, and catchstitch in place.

3. To add a backing, trace around the completed shape on a piece of firmly woven lining fabric and add a ⅝" seam allowance all around.

4. Cut lining, then press seam allowance to wrong side; miter corners and clip curves if necessary.

5. Slipstitch lining in place on back side of needlepoint. Grosgrain ribbon or a strip of felt may be used for a lining on long narrow items like belts.

6. Slipstitch completed appliqué to garment.

Occasionally, canvas edges show when the canvas is turned back to make a belt, pocket or an appliqué. There are three ways to handle this problem.

1. Color the canvas with matching waterproof markers.

2. Enclose the edges with matching or contrasting bias binding. Plan for this from the beginning and work a few extra stitches all around.

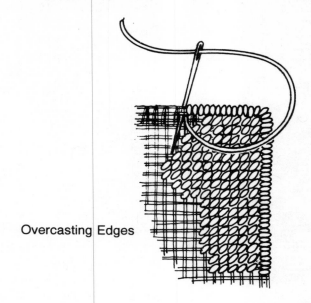

Overcasting Edges

3. On duo (Penelope) canvas, trim canvas leaving three rows of double threads on all sides. Crease canvas back on center pair of threads. Use a double yarn to overcast edges taking a stitch in each hole. Use matching or contrasting yarn.

Filet Crochet

Filet crochet is a durable, easily worked form of lace crochet in which the design is formed with combinations of open squares and solid squares on a chain stitch mesh. Designs are often worked from graphs and many of the cross-stitch and needlepoint designs in this book are suitable for filet crochet.

The designs included in this book are simple ones intended to be worked in strips, squares, or rectangles. Use completed pieces on straps and belts, for patches, pockets, and appliqués or for lace insertions on yokes and sleeves. Strips of filet crochet may also be gathered to use as ruffled edgings.

Materials

Yarns

Yarns vary in size, twist, and texture and many are suitable for filet crochet depending on the desired effect. Yarns such as pearl cotton and "Knit-Cro-Sheen," by Coats and Clark, are ideal for edgings and insertions. Dramatic effects may be created with bulkier acrylic, wool, metallic, and cotton yarns. Since dye lots vary, buy enough for the entire project at the beginning.

Hooks

Crochet hooks are available in a wide variety of sizes made of plastic, metal, or wood. Use steel hooks for work in fine cotton; use plastic, aluminum, or wooden hooks for heavier threads and yarns.

The size of a crocheted piece will depend on the size of the hook and yarn or thread used. A heavy thread will make a much larger piece of the same design than a thread half its size. Measure the garment to determine the exact length needed. Allow for seam allowances and ease. Work a sample and count the number of squares per inch in the sample to calculate the number of squares necessary to reach the desired length. Experiment with thread and various hooks until the proper combination is found. A larger hook will increase the size of the piece, a smaller hook will decrease it.

Crochet Stitches

These are the stitches you will need to execute the filet crochet designs in this book. There are many more. Abbreviations commonly used in crochet directions are:

st.—stitch	dc.—double crochet
ch.—chain	o.—open square
sc.—single crochet	s.—solid square

Foundation Chain

Loop yarn on hook as shown.

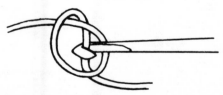

Pull yarn to tighten around hook.

Loop yarn from skein over hook and draw through loop. Repeat until desired length chain is reached.

Single Crochet

Insert hook under two top threads of 2nd chain from hook. Loop yarn from skein over hook.

Draw yarn through stitch. There are now two loops on hook. Loop yarn from skein over hook. Draw through two loops on hook. One loop remains on hook.

Double Crochet

Loop yarn from skein over hook. Insert hook under two top threads of 3rd chain from hook. Loop yarn from skein over hook. Draw yarn through first stitch and loop yarn over hook again.

Draw yarn through two loops. There are now two loops on hook. Loop yarn from skein over hook. Draw yarn through two loops on hook. One loop remains on hook.

Solid And Open Squares

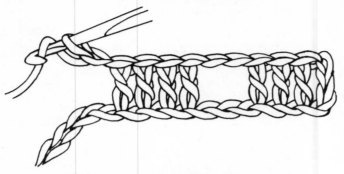

**Read Rows Right To
Left Then Left To Right**

Reading Horizontally

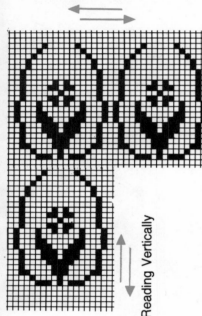

Reading Vertically

Basic Procedure for Filet Crochet

Many of the cross-stitch and needlepoint designs in this book may be worked in filet crochet. In filet crochet, the shapes of a design are defined by open and solid squares. Usually, open squares serve to outline and highlight the design. If you are adapting a cross-stitch or needlepoint design for filet crochet, disregard the color symbols which may appear on the graph. Work out the distribution of open and solid squares on graph paper to define or outline features of the chosen design.

Graph patterns may be followed horizontally or vertically. If there is a repeat, continue until the desired length is reached. A ruler placed on the graph will make following the pattern much easier when working the design. Read rows right to left, then left to right as illustrated. Each row of squares on the graph represents chain or double crochet stitches. Each separate solid square represents four double crochet stitches.

The basic procedure for working filet crochet will be the same for any design, but the distribution of solid and open squares will vary.

1. Make a foundation chain. The length of the chain is three times the number of squares in the row plus six for turning on the first row. For example, a design ten squares wide would require a thirty-six stitch chain.
2. Work the design. *To form the first open square,* work the first double-crochet in the ninth chain from the hook. Do not count the stitch on the hook. *For each subsequent open square,* work one double crochet into the foundation chain, chain two, skip two foundation chains, one double crochet into the next foundation chain. *For each separate solid square,* work four double crochet into the foundation chain. *For two or more consecutive solid squares,* work three double crochet for each and an extra double crochet at the end of the solid area. To turn at the end of a row, add five chains.
3. When work is completed, conceal all ends by running them through several stitches on the wrong side.
4. Clean and steam press into shape.

Instructions for Filet Crochet Butterfly

Instructions for the filet crochet butterfly (design no. 125, page 97) which appears on the cover of this book follow so that you may see how typical filet crochet instructions read. Use this as a guide for interpreting other designs. The butterfly insertion on the cover blouse was worked in "Knit-Cro-Sheen" crochet cotton by Coats and Clark with a no. 8 steel hook.

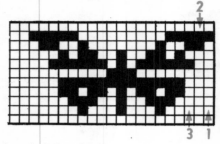

Begin by chaining 39.

Row 1: Work 1 dc. into the 9th chain from the hook to form the first open square, ch. 2, skip 2 st., 1 dc. into the next st. to form the second open square, 7 more o., 1 s., 1 o., 5 ch. turn.

Row 2: Make 1 dc. into last dc. on preceding row, 6 more dc., 8 o., 5 ch. turn.

Row 3: Make 1 dc. into last dc. on preceding row, 5 more o., 1 s., 1 o., 2 s., 1 o., 5 ch. turn.

Follow the diagram making one open square for every white square, and one solid square for every black square. Repeat motif for length desired.

Filet Crochet Edging

Work filet crochet strip in desired length. For a ruffled edging, the finished strip should be two to three times longer than the length needed depending on the desired fullness. Gather the strip to desired length with a running stitch or machine basting along one edge. Use flat edging on straight edges and ruffled edging around curves. It is best to enclose ruffled edgings within a seam for a finished appearance. Choose one of the following methods for attaching edging.

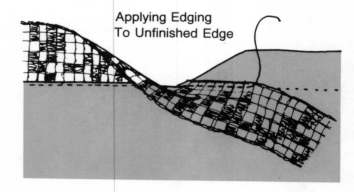

Applying Edging
To Unfinished Edge

Applied Edging On An Unfinished Edge
Use this method to trim an unfinished edge with flat or ruffled edging.

1. Position lace on garment so straight edge is ⅛″ beyond seamline or hemline in seam or hem allowance. Baste in place.
2. Stitch in place by machine.
3. Turn to inside along seamline or hemline, clipping curves whenever necessary. Press.
4. Edgestitch. On inside, turn under raw edges of fabric ¼″ and slipstitch in place.

Applying Edging To Finished Edge

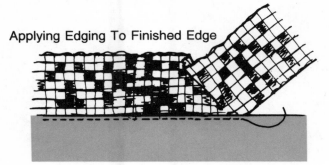

Applied Edging on Finished Edges
Choose this method to attach edging to completed or ready-made garments.
1. Position edging flush with finished garment edge and baste in place. Lap ends that meet in a narrow seam and slipstitch in place. Finish free ends with a narrow hem, if necessary.
2. Sew in place by hand with tiny backstitches or overcasting.

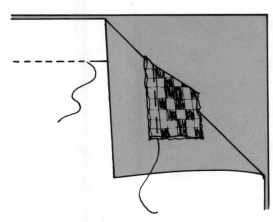

Enclosed Edging

Enclosed Edging
Use this method to sandwich lace between the layers of fabric in collars, cuffs, and ordinary seams.
1. Place edge of lace ⅛″ over seamline in seam allowance.
2. Machine baste next to seamline, then pin second fabric layer over first.
3. Stitch alongside basting on seamline.
4. Trim and grade seam allowances. Turn and press, or press seam open and turn lace in desired direction.

Filet Crochet Insertion and Appliqué

Filet crochet may be added to existing garments or included in the construction of new ones as insertion or appliqué.

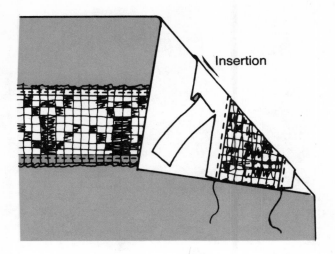

Insertion

Insertion
1. Determine placement lines for insertion and mark them on pattern piece. Transfer to fabric with thread basting. On finished garments, mark fabric lightly with dressmaker's chalk, then thread baste on lines.
2. To determine required length of filet crochet, measure placement lines. Vertical bands of insertion should be planned to extend into the hem allowance for a finished appearance. Ends of strips should extend into seam allowances. Add ½″ seam allowances wherever needed.
3. Complete crocheted strip in required length and baste to garment along positioning lines. On ready-made clothing, open garment seams wherever necessary to enclose ends of insertion. Resew seams after insertion is completed.
4. Cut away fabric between placement lines to within ½″ of the basting and press raw edges away from insertion. To prevent stretching and for added support, insertion can be lined with a firm, sheer fabric like organza in a matching, contrasting, or skin tone color. Cut lining strip 1″ larger than insertion all around and position it under insertion with ½″ extending on each edge. Baste in place.
5. On the right side of garment, machine edgestitch insertion along basting. Catch folded edges and lining (if used) as you stitch. Remove basting and press lightly.

Appliqué
1. Work crochet in desired size and shape.
2. Mark placement lines as outlined in step 1, above.
3. Pin or baste crocheted piece in position on placement lines, then stitch in place by hand or machine.
4. Remove basting and press.

Index

A

Alphabets, historical notes and design plates, 100–105
Appliqué, historical notes and design plates, 72–80
Appliqué, materials and techniques, 116–118
    basic procedure, 116–117
    embroidery as, 109
    filet crochet, 127
    floating, 118
    fusible, 117
    needlepoint, 124
    raw edge, 117
    reverse, 117–118
    shadow, 118
    turned edge, 116–117

B

Basting, grid, 114; radial, 114
Beading, historical notes and design plates, 58–62
Beading materials and techniques, 112–113
    basic procedures, 113
    needlepoint, 123
    stitches, 113
Blocking, 14
Braiding, historical notes and design plates, 63–67
Braiding, materials and techniques, 111–112
    basic procedure, 112

C

Canvas, needlepoint, 121
Corners, mitering, 112, 116
Crochet stitches, 125–126
    double crochet, 125
    foundation chain, 125
    open squares, 126
    single crochet, 125
    solid squares, 126
Curves, clipping, 116

D

Design placement and adaptation, 10–11
Design plates and historical notes, 33–105
Direct tracing on tissue paper, 13
Dressmaker's carbon tracing, 13

E

Edging, 126–127
    applied, finished edge, 127
    applied, unfinished edge, 126–127
    enclosed, 127
Embroidery, historical notes and design plates, 33–53
Embroidery, materials and techniques, 106–110
    basic procedure, 106–107
    cross-stitch, 109; on canvas, 109–110
    hoop, 107
    knits, on, 108
    mirrors, with, 108–109
    stitches, 107–108
        backstitch, 107
        blanket stitch, 107
        buttonhole scallop, 108
        chain stitch, 107
        couching, 107
        cross-stitch, 108
        duplicate stitch, 108
        eyelet, 108; padded, 108
        feather stitch, 108
        French knot, 108
        French stemming, 107
        herringbone stitch, 108
        lazy daisy, 107
        long and short stitch, 108
        outline stitch (see stem stitch)
        running stitch, 107
        satin stitch, 108; padded, 108
        seed stitch, 107
        stem stitch, 107
Enclosed edging, 127
Enlarging and reducing designs, 12

F

Filet crochet, historical notes and design plates, 96–99
Filet crochet, materials and techniques, 124–127
    appliqué, 127
    basic procedure, 126
    edging, 126–127
    insertion, 127
Floating appliqué, 118
Fusible appliqué, 117
Fusibles, 116

H

Hand sewing needles, 107
Hooks, crochet, 125
Hoop, embroidery, 107; quilting, 114
Hot iron transfer pencil, 13

K

Knits, embroidery on, 108

M

Mirrors, embroidery with, 108–109
Mitering, 112, 116
Monograms, 100

N

Needlepoint, historical notes and design plates, 86–95
Needlepoint, materials and techniques, 120–124
    appliqué, 124
    basic procedure, 122–123
    beading, 123
    binding canvas, 122
    canvas, 121
    cloth, 123–124
    edge finishes, 124
    stitches, 121
        basketweave stitch, 121
        brick stitch, 121
        byzantine stitch, 121
        continental stitch, 121
        cross-stitch, 121
        half cross-stitch, 121
        mosaic stitch, 121
Needles, hand sewing, 107

P

Patchwork, historical notes and design plates, 81–85
Patchwork, materials and techniques, 119–120
    applied, 120
    basic procedure, 119–120
    garments and sections, 120
    hand piecing, 120
    machine piecing, 120
Preliminary planning, 10
Project sequence, 11–12
Punch-work, historical notes and design plates, 54–57
Punch-work, materials and techniques, 110–111
    basic procedure, 110
    stitch, 110–111

Q

Quilting, historical notes and design plates, 68–71
Quilting, materials and techniques, 113–115
    basic procedure, 114–115
    completed garments, on, 115
    hand, 114
    machine, 115

R

Ready-made clothing, needlework on (see individual needlework techniques)
Reducing and enlarging designs, 12
Reverse appliqué, 117–118

S

Selection of materials and techniques, 11
Shadow appliqué, 118
Shi-sha (Shiska) embroidery, 108–109
Stitches, beading, 113
    crochet, 125–126
    embroidery, 107–108
    needlepoint, 121

T

Templates, 14
Thread tracing, 13
Transferring designs to fabric, 12–14
    direct tracing on tissue paper, 13
    dressmaker's carbon tracing, 13
    hot iron transfer pencil, 13
    templates, 14
    thread tracing, 14
Trapunto, materials and techniques, 115–116
    basic procedure, 115–116
    ready-made clothing, on, 116